Language Arts
Resources from Recyclables

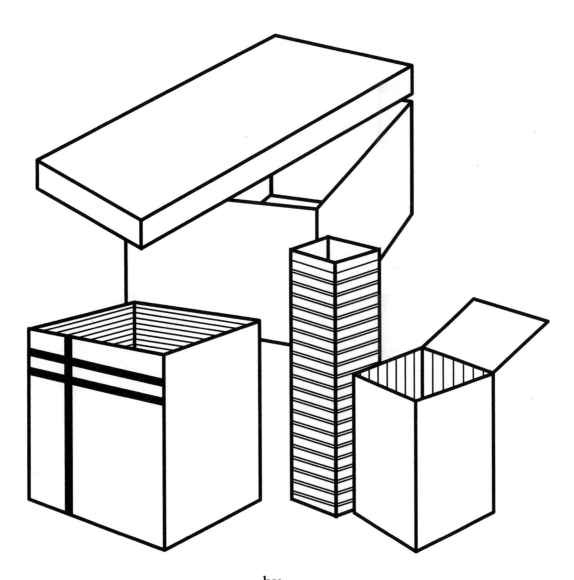

by
Bonnie Mertzlufft • Brenda Morton • Virginia Woolf

illustrated by
Susan Pinkerton

Publisher: *Roberta Suid*
Editor: *Carol Whiteley*
Design and Production: *Susan Pinkerton*
Cover design: *Terrence Meagher*
Consultants: *Catherine Dilts* and *Lillian Lieberman*

For a complete catalog please write to the address below.
Monday Morning Books
P.O. Box 1680, Palo Alto, CA 94302

ISBN 1-878279-71-8

Printed in the United States of America

987654321

CONTENTS

INTRODUCTION

Language Arts Resources from Recyclables brings the concepts of recycling and educating together. This book focuses on reusing materials in activities and projects that further children's reading, writing, and language skills. By making learning tools from throwaways, you will be conserving your own time and energy while helping to save the environment. Most of the projects in this book may be "recycled" in your own classroom in the years ahead.

As you flip through the pages of *Language Arts Resources from Recyclables*, you will notice the easy-to-follow manner in which the projects are presented. Each activity includes a list of materials, detailed directions for constructing the item, and suggested methods for use with students in your classroom. Reproducible patterns, word lists, samples, and illustrations are also provided throughout the book.

Language Arts Resources from Recyclables is divided into thirteen chapters. Each chapter is devoted to the use of a different recyclable material, including construction paper scraps, small milk cartons, egg cartons, Popsicle sticks, small boxes, and more. The activities in each chapter cover four levels of skill development, geared toward the primary grades (K-3). However, you should not feel limited by the grades suggested on the activity pages. Many of the projects can easily be adapted to fit the needs of other grade levels, other subjects across the curriculum, or children with special needs.

As a concerned educator, you have probably looked for breaks from a daily paper/pencil classroom routine. These activities will help involve students in the learning process by encouraging them to manipulate activity pieces, cut, paste, work creatively, and more. The students will be able to work away from their desks on many of the projects. Use the floor, the reading table, or the bulletin board as alternate working surfaces to make the school day more fun and interesting for your students.

Your reward from using the activities in *Language Arts Resources from Recyclables* is three-fold! You will be helping the environment by recycling, saving your own time by creating long-lasting learning equipment, and, most importantly, watching your students achieve in reading, writing, and language skills.

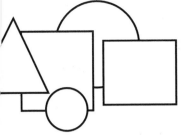

PARENT LETTER

Note to Teacher:
Duplicate this letter and place a check mark beside the items you need. Send the letter home with your students.

Dear Parents,
   We are making tools from recyclables to use in our classroom. If you have any of the following items, please send them to school as soon as possible.

_____ milk jug caps (all colors)
_____ Styrofoam meat trays (all sizes and colors)
_____ old magazines
_____ large paper grocery bags
_____ empty boxes (all shapes and sizes)
_____ old calendars
_____ newspapers
_____ used wrapping paper
_____ Popsicle sticks
_____ cardboard egg cartons
_____ used greeting cards

   If you are available to help assemble resources or work with children in the classroom, please mark the appropriate spaces below.

_____ I can help at school (____ mornings/____evenings).
_____ I can help at home.
The best day for me is _____.

Thank you!

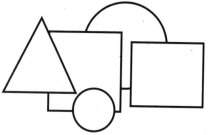

PARENT THANK YOU NOTE

Note to Teacher:

Duplicate this thank you card onto colored paper. Send it home with children who have brought supply materials for the recycling projects. You might also send it to parents or guardians who have donated their time to help.

Recycling Counts!
I was glad I could count
on you. Thank you.

_____

teacher signature

CHAPTER ONE

MILK JUG CAPS

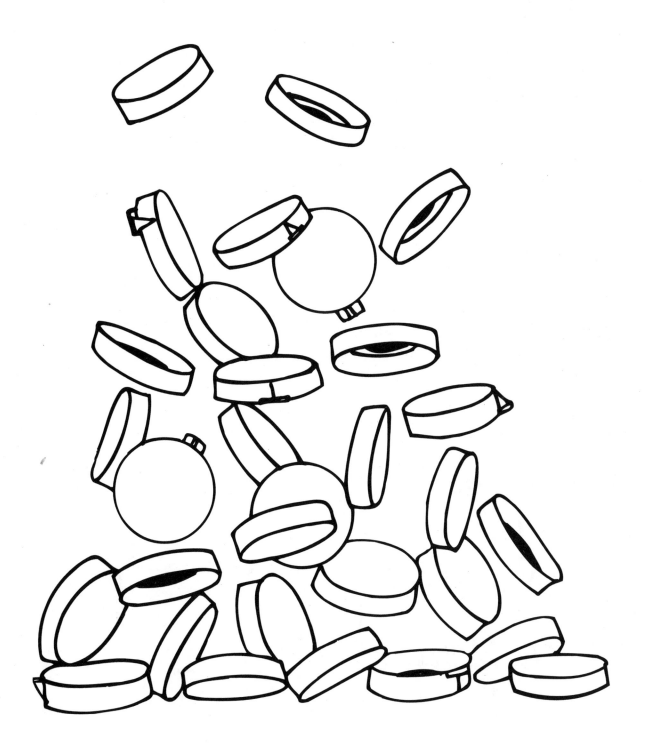

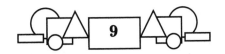

CLASSIFICATION

Objective: To sort pictures into classification groups.

Materials: milk jug caps in sets of 12 (if possible, use same-colored caps in each set), classification patterns (pg. 11), tape, small plastic bags, scissors, tagboard, glue

Construction:
1. Cut out the patterns, mount on tagboard, laminate, and cut out again.
2. Tape one pattern to each milk jug cap.
3. Store each set of caps in a plastic bag.

Directions for Student:
1. Spread out all the caps on a table.
2. Sort the pictures into classification sets: animals, food, clothes; or vehicles, body parts, furniture.

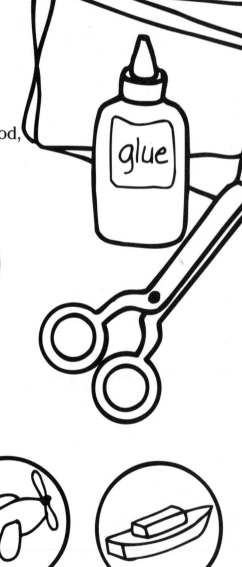

10

CLASSIFICATION PATTERNS

11

LONG/SHORT VOWEL SOUNDS

FIRST GRADE

Objective: To master long and short vowel sounds.

Materials: 30 milk jug caps, word patterns (pg. 13), tagboard, small plastic bag, scissors, tape, marker

Construction:
1. Laminate the word circles, cut out, and tape one to each milk jug cap.
2. Write the words "Long" and "Short" on two pieces of tagboard.
3. Store caps and long and short vowel cards in a plastic bag.

Directions for Student:
1. Place the long and short vowel cards on a flat surface.
2. Sort the caps and place them under the correct vowel sound card.

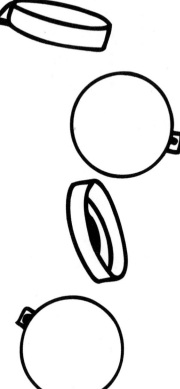

FIRST GRADE PATTERNS

SHORT

bat cap sack egg ten

inch fish pick sock mop

box cup duck rust pet

LONG

came face rake meet queen

we mile kite bike tote

toe row mute cube mule

13

SECOND GRADE

Objective: To reinforce alphabetization skills.

Materials: 25 milk jug caps, word patterns (pg. 15), tape, small plastic bag, scissors

Construction:
1. Laminate and cut out the word circles.
2. Tape one word circle to each milk jug cap.
3. Store in a plastic bag.

Directions for Student:
1. Sort the milk jug caps into piles of five according to the beginning letter of each word.
2. Then, arrange each set in alphabetical order according to the second letter in each word.

Option: Create additional sets for more- or less-advanced students by writing your own words on paper circles, laminating, and taping to caps.

14

SECOND GRADE PATTERNS

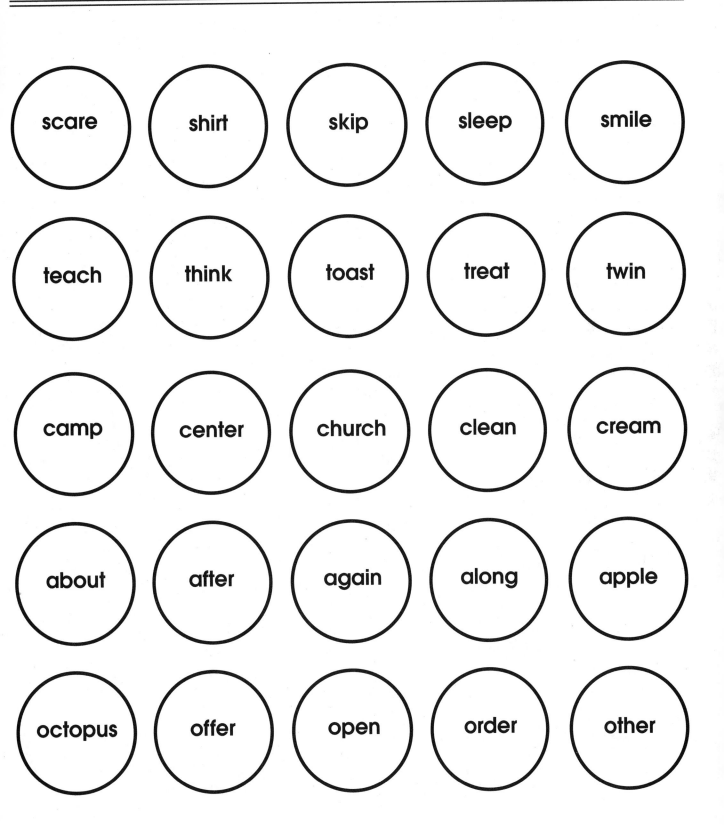

scare   shirt   skip   sleep   smile

teach   think   toast   treat   twin

camp   center   church   clean   cream

about   after   again   along   apple

octopus   offer   open   order   other

DICTIONARY HUNT

THIRD GRADE

Objective: To reinforce dictionary skills and to master vocabulary.

Materials: milk jug caps in sets of 10 (make sets to use with small groups), cap-sized construction paper circles, worksheet (pg. 17), sample word lists (pg. 18), marker, tape, small plastic bags, scissors, dictionary

Construction:
1. Write a word on each circle, making sure that the words can be found in your school dictionary. (Select the words at random, or choose from a story, social studies unit, or science chapter.)
2. Number the words in each set from 1 to 10.
3. Laminate all the circles, cut them out, and tape the circles to the caps.
4. Store the caps in plastic bags in sets of 10.
5. Make an answer key by looking up the words in the dictionary and writing the word, page number, and definition.
6. Duplicate the worksheet for student use.

Directions for Student:
1. Pick a word from a plastic bag and write it by the matching number on the worksheet.
2. Look up the word in the dictionary and write down the page number and definition.
3. When you have looked up all the words in the bag, get the answer key from the teacher and check your answers.

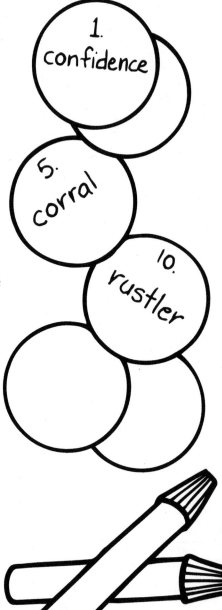

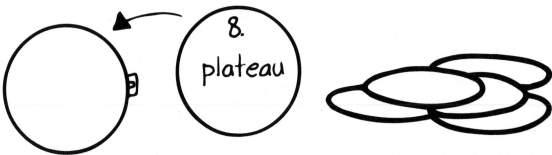

DICTIONARY HUNT

1. _____ pg. _____

_____

_____

2. _____ pg. _____

_____

_____

3. _____ pg. _____

_____

_____

4. _____ pg. _____

_____

_____

5. _____ pg. _____

_____

_____

6. _____ pg. _____

_____

_____

7. _____ pg. _____

_____

_____

8. _____ pg. _____

_____

_____

9. _____ pg. _____

_____

_____

10. _____ pg. _____

_____

SAMPLE WORD LISTS

List One:
Me and My Little Brain
by John D. Fitzgerald

1. bamboozled
2. confidence
3. corral
4. edition
5. epidemic
6. imitate
7. plateau
8. prospector
9. revenge
10. rustler

List Two:
Ramona Quimby, Age 8
by Beverly Cleary

1. accuracy
2. assigned
3. consideration
4. ferocious
5. intermediate
6. reassuring
7. responsibility
8. satisfied
9. suspicious
10. wistfully

CHAPTER TWO

STYROFOAM MEAT TRAYS

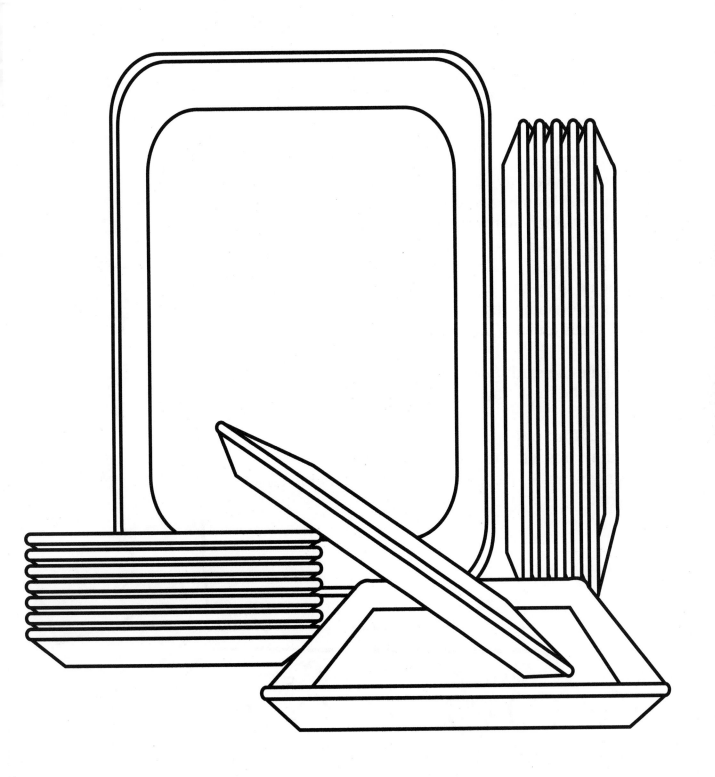

KINDERGARTEN

Objective: To master same and different identification.

Materials: one large meat tray (to hold two sets of sorting cards), same/different patterns (pg. 21), colored markers, scissors, permanent marker, large plastic bag

Construction:
1. Divide the meat tray and use the permanent marker to label one half "Same" and the other half "Different."
2. Use the permanent marker to draw two like objects on the "Same" half and two different objects on the "Different" half.
3. Duplicate the same and different patterns, cut them out, and color in the objects using the same colors for the "Same" cards and two different colors for the "Different" cards.
4. Laminate the cards and store them in a plastic bag along with the meat tray.

Directions for Student:
1. Sort the cards into the correct side of the meat tray.
2. When you finish, show the tray to the teacher to check your work.

SAME/DIFFERENT PATTERNS

RHYMING DOMINOES

FIRST GRADE

Objective: To read and recognize words that sound alike.

Materials: enough meat trays to cut out 24 dominoes (to fit domino patterns), domino patterns (pg. 23), large plastic bag, scissors, glue

Construction:
1. Duplicate the dominoes and cut out.
2. Use the domino patterns to cut trays into the correct sized dominoes.
3. Glue the patterns to the meat tray dominoes.
4. Store all pieces in a plastic bag.

Directions for Two Students:
1. Divide the dominoes and turn them face down.
2. Place one domino face up on the table.
3. Take turns flipping over one domino and putting it into play if one of its words rhymes with the word on the open end of a domino on the table. Play again if there is a rhyme.
4. If there is no rhyme, turn the domino back over and let your partner take a turn.
5. The player who runs out of dominoes first wins!

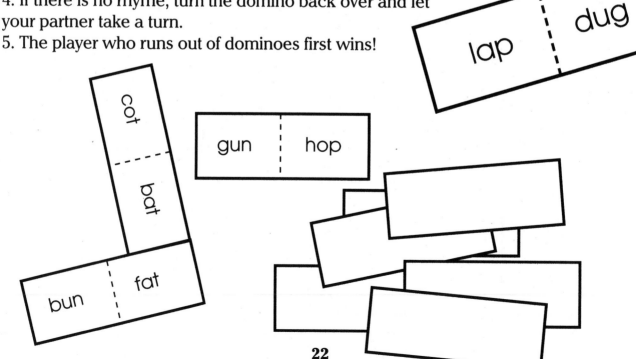

DOMINO PATTERNS

bun	fat

bag	men

wet	pop

not	rug

bit	bug

cap	log

gun	hop

rag	tug

sat	net

cot	bat

sit	chin

tap	win

DOMINO PATTERNS

sun	hen

tag	top

get	tin

hot	pen

hit	ten

lap	dug

run	dog

sag	mop

pet	hog

pot	sin

kit	fog

map	cat

BOOK COVERS FOR STORIES

SECOND GRADE

Objective: To identify the theme of a story by making a book cover for it.

Materials: meat trays (two per child), white paper, one piece of construction paper, pencils, crayons, markers, hole punch, yarn scraps, clear Contact paper, shape patterns (pgs. 26-27), glue, scissors,

Construction:
1. Use the patterns to cut the two trays into the shape each child has chosen.
2. Cut several pages of the white paper in the same shapes and assemble them between the two meat tray covers.
3. Punch two holes along one side of the meat trays and the pages.
4. Bind the book together with the scraps of yarn.
5. Help the child cover the completed book with clear Contact paper.

Directions for Student:
1. Choose a cover and write a story on the pages of the book.
2. Cut a piece of construction paper into the same shape as the meat tray.
3. Glue the cover onto the top meat tray.
4. Write a title for your story and decorate the paper cover so it suits the story.
5. Share your book with your classmates.

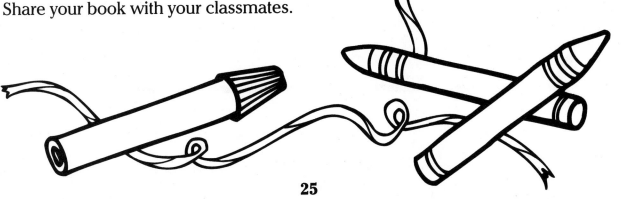

SHAPE PATTERNS

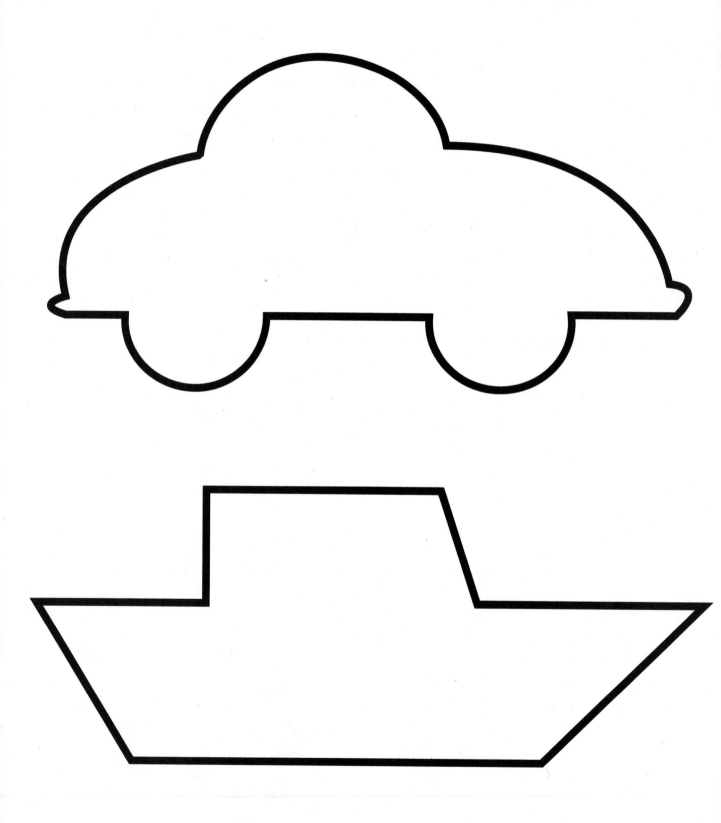

SHAPE PATTERNS

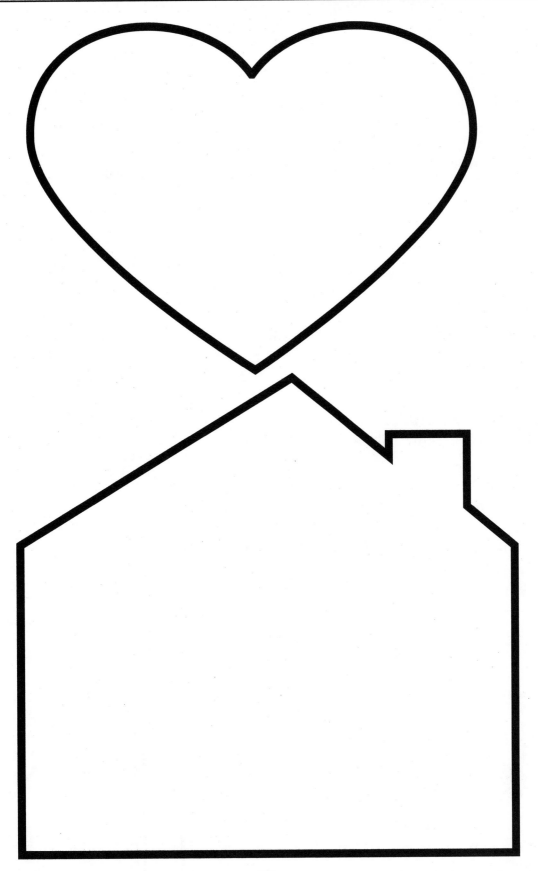

PARTS OF SPEECH

THIRD GRADE

Objective: To master the parts of speech.

Materials: 5 meat trays, sample sentence sheets (pgs. 29 - 30), marker, pencil, golf tee for each set made, plastic bags

Construction:
1. Write four sample sentences on each meat tray and put the speech part answer choices under each sentence.
2. Poke a hole above each speech part word using a pencil. (See the illustration.)
3. On the back of each meat tray, circle the correct hole for the checker.
4. Store materials in plastic bags.

Directions for Two Students:
1. Decide which person will be the worker and which the checker.
2. The checker holds the meat tray at arm's length while the worker pokes the golf tee into the hole that indicates the part of speech of the underlined word.
3. If the golf tee shows through the hole that is circled, then the worker is correct. Otherwise, the checker tells the worker to try again.
4. Get another tray and change jobs.

The pig was in the <u>red</u> barn.

   O   O   O   O

noun   verb   adjective   adverb

SAMPLE SENTENCES

The pig was in the <u>red</u> barn.
noun verb **adjective** adverb

The duck <u>slowly</u> waddled away.
noun verb pronoun **adverb**

<u>She</u> has a pink dress.
verb adverb **pronoun** adjective

The hot <u>coffee</u> steamed.
verb adverb pronoun **noun**

The <u>fox</u> ran to his den.
verb **noun** adverb adjective

The table has a <u>crooked</u> leg.
adjective noun adverb verb

My dad can <u>hardly</u> whistle.
adjective **adverb** noun pronoun

Their dog <u>chased</u> me.
noun pronoun **verb** adjective

I watched a <u>scary</u> movie.
pronoun adverb **adjective** noun

The dog <u>growled</u> at us.
noun adverb adjective **verb**

SAMPLE SENTENCES

The snowman <u>melted</u> in the sun.
noun adverb **verb** adjective

The <u>television</u> control was broken.
noun verb **adjective** pronoun

<u>His</u> hot dog dropped on the ground.
pronoun verb adjective adverb

<u>Our</u> house is next to the store.
noun verb **pronoun** adverb

The children read <u>quietly</u>.
noun pronoun verb **adverb**

He saw a beautiful <u>rainbow</u>.
pronoun **noun** verb adjective

The bird sang <u>sweetly</u>.
noun adjective **adverb** verb

Jack's <u>truck</u> broke down.
pronoun **noun** adjective verb

The thunder crashed <u>loudly</u>.
noun pronoun **adverb** adjective

The <u>cookies</u> smelled good.
noun pronoun adjective verb.

CHAPTER THREE

SMALL MILK CARTONS

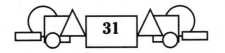

PHONICS COLLAGE

KINDERGARTEN

Objective: To reinforce beginning sounds of words.

Materials: one small clean milk carton with the top cut off per child, old magazines, glue, letter patterns (pg. 33), scissors

Construction:
1. Turn each milk carton upside down so the flat bottom is the top.
2. Reproduce the letter patterns and cut apart.
3. Glue a letter on the top of each milk carton.
4. Give a carton to each student.
5. Set out the magazines, scissors, and glue.

Directions for Student:
1. Find and cut out four pictures that begin with the same letter as the one on your carton.
2. Glue one picture to each side of the milk carton.

Option: As a homework activity, ask the students to complete their letter collection by finding at least one small object at home that begins with their letter and bringing it to school in their milk carton collage.

cut

LETTER PATTERNS

A B C D E F
G H I J K L
M N O P Q
R S T U V W
X Y Z

SINGULAR AND PLURAL

FIRST GRADE

Objective: To master the difference between singular and plural.

Materials: two small milk cartons for each set of singular/plural cards made, tagboard, colored Contact paper, scissors, stapler, plastic bags, glue, sail patterns and word cards (pg. 35)

Construction:
1. Open the two milk cartons to make boats and cut off the tops. (See illustration.)
2. Cover the boxes on all four sides with colored Contact paper.
3. Duplicate the sail patterns onto tagboard, cut them out, and glue or staple one sail to the front of each "boat."
4. Place the singular and plural boats side by side.
5. Duplicate the singular and plural word cards and laminate them.
6. Place the cards in a plastic bag and store in one of the boats.

Directions for Student:
1. Read the words on the cards.
2. Find the singular and plural word cards. (Singular means "one" and plural means "more than one.")
3. Place the cards into the correct boats.

remove top and attach sail

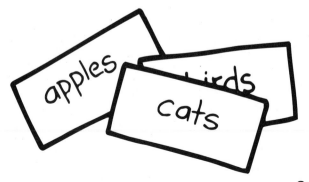

34

SAIL PATTERNS AND WORD CARDS

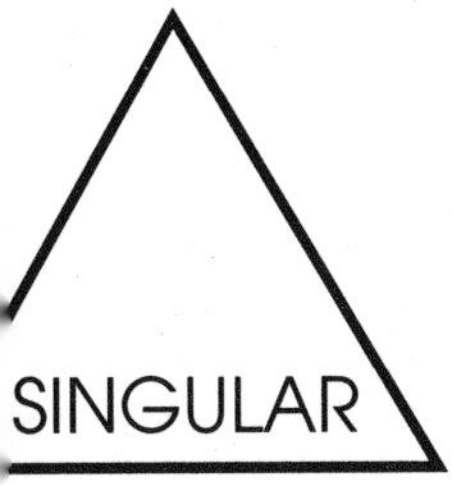

△
SINGULAR

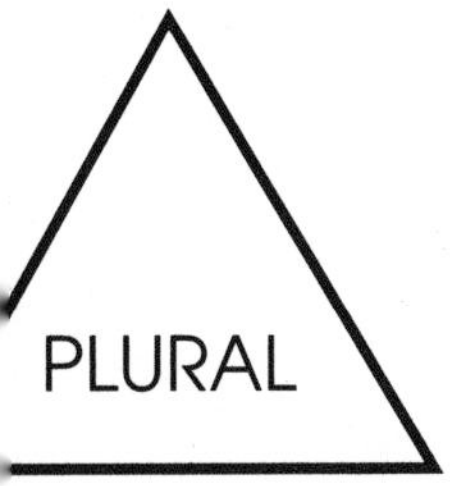

man	woman	child
boat	cat	book
flower	bird	apple
foot		men
women	children	boats

△
PLURAL

| cats | books | flowers |
| birds | apples | feet |

SYNONYMS AND ANTONYMS

SECOND GRADE

Objective: To reinforce the concepts of synonyms and antonyms.

Materials: two small milk cartons, marker, colored Contact paper, scissors, glue or stapler, synonym and antonym word cards (pg. 37), plastic bag

Construction:
1. Cut off the tops of the two milk cartons to make boxes.
2. Cover the milk cartons on all four sides with colored Contact paper.
3. Write "Same" on the side of one box and "Opposite" on the other box.
4. Glue or staple the boxes together to make one box with two top openings.
5. Duplicate the word cards, laminate, and cut apart.
6. Store the word cards in a plastic bag in one side of the box.

Directions for Student:
1. Read the word pairs on each card and decide whether the words mean the same thing or whether they mean two different things.
2. Insert the cards into the correct side of the box.

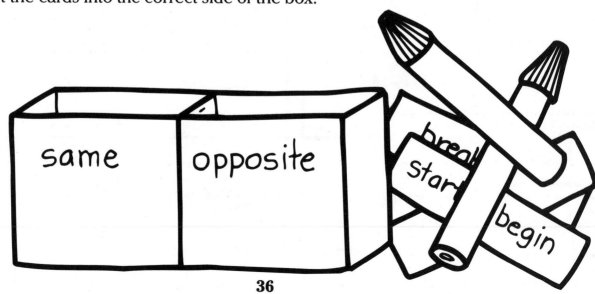

SYNONYM AND ANTONYM WORD CARDS

SYNONYMS

sick ill	leave go	shout yell
mend fix	start begin	kind nice
touch feel	autumn fall	cut chop
small little	big large	smile grin
glad happy	beautiful pretty	absent gone

ANTONYMS

sick well	leave stay	shout whisper
break fix	start finish	polite rude
tall short	grin frown	win lose
small large	boy girl	summer winter
happy sad	beautiful ugly	absent present

FACT AND OPINION

THIRD GRADE

Objective: To understand the difference between facts and opinions.

Materials: two small milk cartons, sample sentence strips (pg. 39), fact/opinion worksheet (pg. 40), tagboard strips, stapler, colored Contact paper, scissors, marker, plastic bag, writing paper, pencils

Construction:
1. Duplicate the sample sentences onto tagboard strips, laminate, and cut out. Store in the bag.
2. Cut off the tops of the milk cartons.
3. Staple the milk carton "boxes" together.
4. Cover with colored Contact paper.
5. Write the word "Fact" on the front of one box and "Opinion" on the other.
6. Duplicate the worksheets.

Directions for Student:
1. Choose five sentences and decide if each is a fact or an opinion and place it in the correct milk carton section.
2. Write the sentences under the correct column on the worksheet. Turn the paper in to your teacher to be corrected.

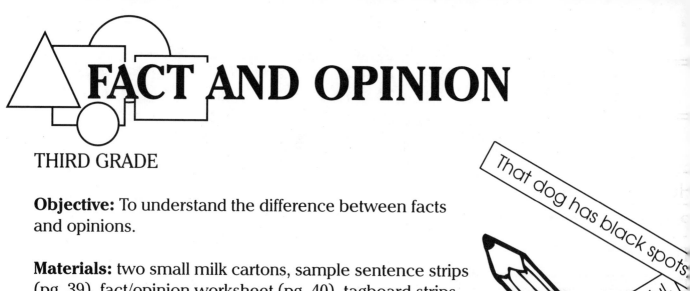

SAMPLE SENTENCE STRIPS

Her house is blue and has white shutters.   (F)

Pam's house is not as pretty as mine.   (O)

The rock fell on my foot.   (F)

That rock is ugly.   (O)

That dog has black spots.   (F)

My dog is the most beautiful dog in the world.   (O)

The car has a flat tire.   (F)

His new car cost too much.   (O)

Jack scored ten points in his last game.   (F)

Jack is a better player than Jim.   (O)

Polly has red hair.   (F)

Polly's hair is beautiful.   (O)

The referee called a foul on Tom.   (F)

The referee called too many fouls on our team.   (O)

Jim has seven letters in his last name.   (F)

His last name is too hard to say.   (O)

The clown has a purple hat.   (F)

The clown has a funny suit.   (O)

I have two pickles on my hamburger.   (F)

These pickles are too sour.   (O)

O = Opinion
F = Fact
Note: This is an answer key. Remove the F's and O's before giving the
sentence strips to the children.

Name: _____

FACT OR OPINION

FACT

1. _____

_____

2. _____

_____

3. _____

_____

4. _____

_____

5. _____

_____

OPINION

1. _____

_____

2. _____

_____

3. _____

_____

4. _____

_____

5. _____

_____

CHAPTER FOUR

OLD MAGAZINES

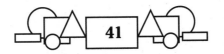

SPELL IT OUT

KINDERGARTEN

Objective: To practice spelling simple words.

Materials: old magazines, scissors, glue, tagboard, marker, small plastic bags

Construction:
1. Cut simple pictures from magazines—pictures that show one obvious item: cat, tree, house, apple, etc.
2. Glue the pictures to pieces of tagboard.
3. Use three pictures to spell out a word: house, apple, tree = hat.
4. Write a number on the bottom of each picture to help children put the cards in order: house = 1, apple = 2, tree = 3.
5. Store each set of cards in a separate bag.

Directions for Student:
1. Spread the pictures on a flat surface.
2. Name the objects in the pictures and then put them in order by the numbers on the bottom.
3. Say the first letter of each object, and spell out the word that the letters make.

SCAVENGER HUNT

FIRST GRADE

Objective: To learn to follow written directions.

Materials: scavenger hunt lists (pg. 44), old magazines (one for each child), scissors, glue, construction paper

Construction:
1. Duplicate the scavenger hunt lists.
2. Divide the students into groups of three or four and give each group a list of items to find in the magazines.

Directions for Student:
1. Look through the magazines and find pictures of the items on the list.
2. Cut the pictures out and paste them on construction paper.

SCAVENGER HUNT LISTS

LIST 1

1. house
2. cat
3. red car
4. child
5. book or newspaper

LIST 2

1. swimming pool
2. dog
3. truck
4. fruit or vegetable
5. woman

LIST 3

1. airplane
2. table
3. shoe
4. man
5. box

LIST 4

1. tree
2. truck
3. chair
4. flower
5. dish

WHO SAID IT?

SECOND GRADE

Objective: To reinforce reading comprehension skills.

Materials: 10 pictures cut from old magazines, tagboard, scissors, markers, glue, plastic bag

Construction:
1. Glue each picture onto a piece of tagboard.
2. Write an accompanying sentence that tells what the person or object in the picture might be saying.
3. Laminate the pictures and sentences, cut out, and store in a plastic bag.
4. Make an answer key showing which pictures go with which sentences.

Directions for Student:
1. Look at the picture cards and sentence strips.
2. Try to match each picture with the correct sentence strip.
3. Check your answers with the key.

Let's eat dinner.

I want to play ball.

Let's take a plane!

READING COMPREHENSION

THIRD GRADE

Objective: To reinforce reading comprehension skills.

Materials: 10 pictures cut from magazines, 10 pieces of tagboard large enough for 1 magazine picture and 4 sentences, markers, washable crayons or felt pens, glue, plastic bag

Construction:
1. Mount a picture at the top of each piece of tagboard.
2. Write four sentences under the picture. (Only one sentence should be completely true according to the picture; the others may be partly true.)
3. Laminate the cards so that the children can use a washable crayon or felt pen to underline answers.
4. Either write an answer key for children to use to check themselves, or collect cards and check after student use.
5. Store the cards in the bag.

Fish use gills to breathe.

Directions for Student:
1. Take out a card and look at the picture.
2. Read the sentences and decide which one sentence is exactly true.
3. Underline that sentence with a washable crayon or felt pen.
4. Choose the correct sentence for the rest of the pictures in the bag.

CHAPTER FIVE

CONSTRUCTION PAPER SCRAPS

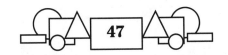

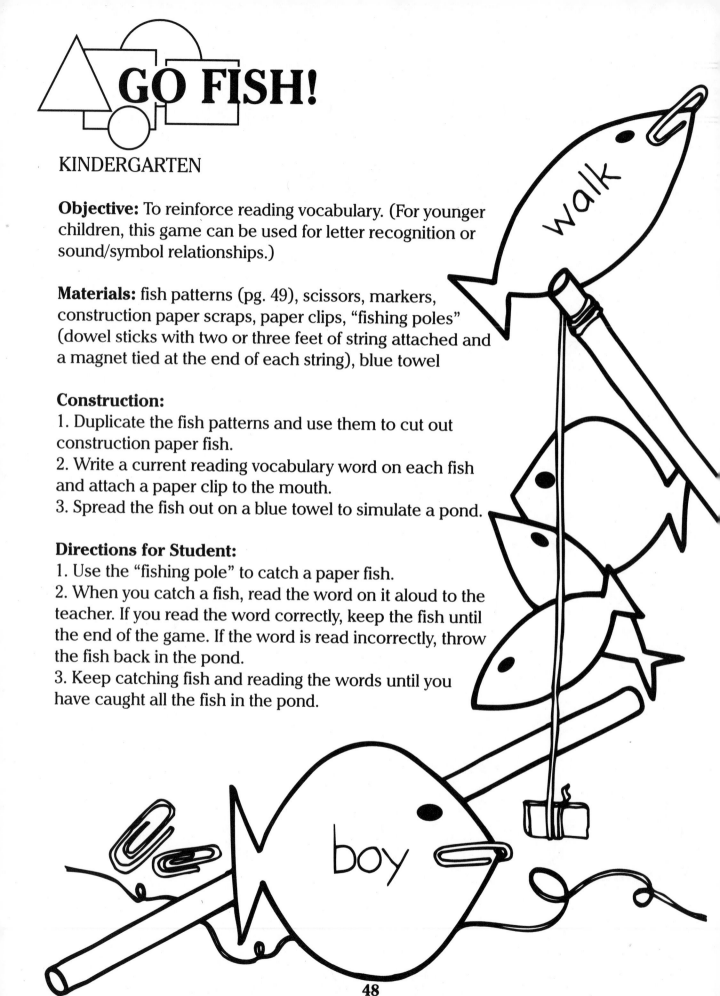

GO FISH!

KINDERGARTEN

Objective: To reinforce reading vocabulary. (For younger children, this game can be used for letter recognition or sound/symbol relationships.)

Materials: fish patterns (pg. 49), scissors, markers, construction paper scraps, paper clips, "fishing poles" (dowel sticks with two or three feet of string attached and a magnet tied at the end of each string), blue towel

Construction:
1. Duplicate the fish patterns and use them to cut out construction paper fish.
2. Write a current reading vocabulary word on each fish and attach a paper clip to the mouth.
3. Spread the fish out on a blue towel to simulate a pond.

Directions for Student:
1. Use the "fishing pole" to catch a paper fish.
2. When you catch a fish, read the word on it aloud to the teacher. If you read the word correctly, keep the fish until the end of the game. If the word is read incorrectly, throw the fish back in the pond.
3. Keep catching fish and reading the words until you have caught all the fish in the pond.

FISH PATTERNS

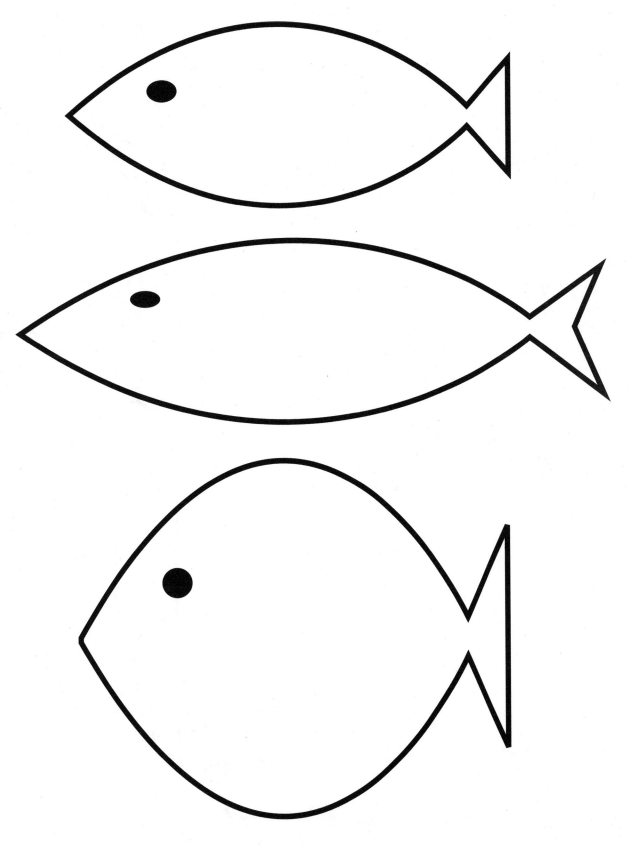

COLOR WORDS

FIRST GRADE

Objective: To reinforce the recognition and spelling of color words.

Materials: construction paper scraps in various colors, crayon and box patterns (pg. 51), tagboard, scissors, markers, glue

Construction:
1. Duplicate the crayon and box patterns onto tagboard for the children to use as stencils. Make enough for your class to share.
2. Assemble the supplies.
3. Write the color words on the board—or have the children look at their own real crayons to find out how to spell the color words.

Directions for Student:
1. Choose three different colors of construction paper.
2. Use the crayon pattern to trace a crayon on each piece of paper. Cut the crayon shapes out.
3. Use a marker to write the name of the color on each paper crayon.
4. Use the box pattern to trace and then cut out a crayon box shape.
5. Glue the paper crayons to the box shape to make a box of crayons.
6. You may continue making more paper crayons until the box is full.

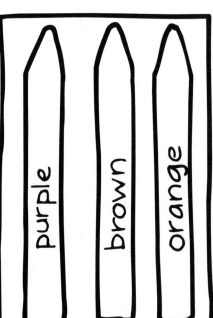

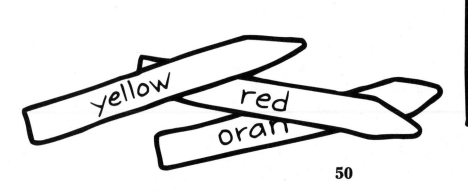

CRAYON AND BOX PATTERNS

FRIENDSHIP CHAINS

SECOND GRADE

Objective: To brainstorm and describe a friend's good qualities.

Materials: construction paper scraps, scissors, markers, stapler or glue, small strips of note paper, empty coffee can or shoe box

Construction:
1. Write the name of each student on one of the small strips of note paper and place the strips in an empty coffee can or shoe box.
2. Tell the students that they are going to make Friendship Chains from scrap paper.
3. Explain that the chains will each have five links that tell something nice about one person.

Directions for Student:
1. Pick a slip of paper from the container of student names.
2. Cut five 1" x 5" strips from various colors of scrap paper.
3. Write one sentence on each strip that tells something positive about the person whose name you picked.
4. Staple the first strip end to end to make a circle. Loop the next strip through the circle and staple its ends together to make another circle. (The two circles will be linked.) Continue with the rest of the five strips to make a chain.
5. Give the chain to the person whose name you chose.

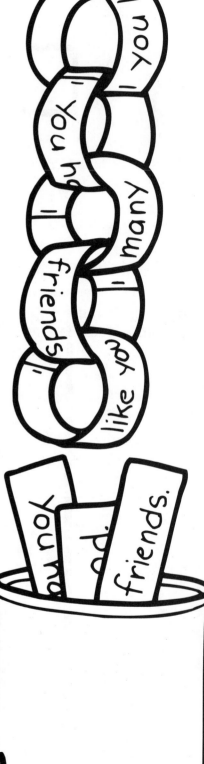

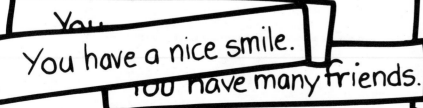

SYNONYM/ANTONYM KITES

THIRD GRADE

Objective: To identify pairs of words as synonyms or antonyms.

Materials: two construction paper kites from pattern (pg. 54), 30 tail sections (pg. 54) cut from various colors of scrap construction paper, two long pieces of yarn or shoestrings, markers, hole punch, scissors

Construction:
1. Write pairs of synonyms on 15 of the kite tail sections and pairs of antonyms on the other 15 tail sections.
2. Write the word "Synonyms" on one kite and "Antonyms" on the other.
3. Laminate all of the pieces and cut them out.
4. Punch holes in each tail section as indicated on the pattern.
5. Attach a length of yarn or a shoestring to each kite.
6. Post the completed kites.

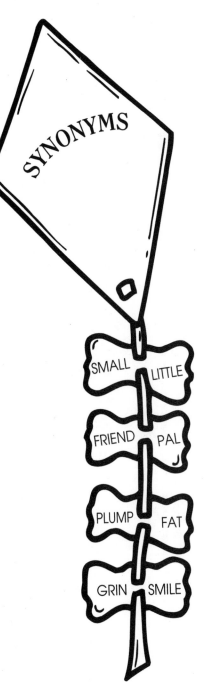

Directions for Student:
1. Take a turn threading all of the pairs of antonyms to the "Antonym" kite, and all of the synonyms to the "Synonym" kite.
2. When everyone has had a chance, the teacher will post the kites on a bulletin board for you to study again.

Option: Advanced students can make their own Antonym and Synonym kites.

KITE PATTERNS

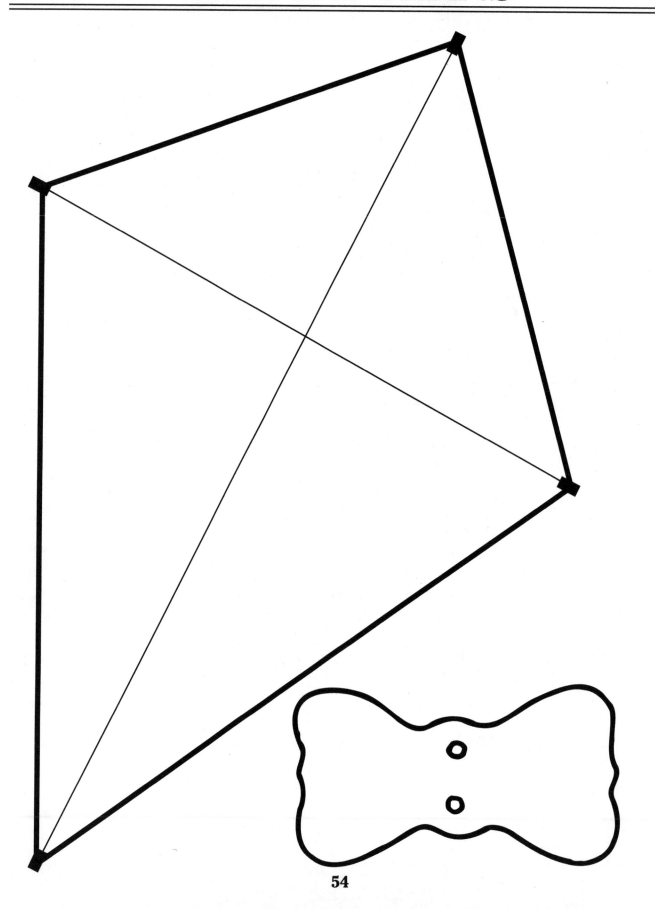

CHAPTER SIX

PAPER BAGS

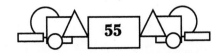

SEASONS COLLAGE

KINDERGARTEN

Objective: To reinforce understanding of the names of the seasons and the type of weather that occurs in each season.

Materials: large paper bag (one per student), scraps of brown and green construction paper, cotton balls, pink tissue paper, markers and crayons, glue, scissors

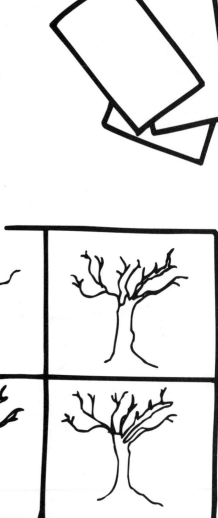

Construction:
1. Cut the bags along the seam so that each child will have a flat surface to work on.
2. Divide each bag into four sections by drawing one line down the middle lengthwise and another crossing it widthwise.
3. After the children complete their trees, help them write the name of the season under each tree.

Directions for Student:
1. Draw a tree in each of the four sections.
2. Decorate the trees according to the four seasons: fall, winter, spring, summer. You can make autumn-colored leaves falling in the first square, glue on cotton balls for winter snow in the second, draw green buds for spring in the third, and glue on pink tissue paper summertime flowers on the tree branches in the fourth.

TRAIN ENGINE AND CARS

FIRST GRADE

Objective: To learn the names and the sequence of the days of the week.

Materials: large paper sacks (one per child), construction paper, engine pattern (pg. 58), train car patterns (pg. 59), tagboard or cardboard, black crayons, markers, scissors, glue

Construction:
1. Cut each sack along the seam so that children have flat surfaces to work on.
2. Duplicate a train engine pattern onto construction paper for each child in the class and cut out.
3. Duplicate the train onto cardboard or tagboard for the children to use as stencils. Cut out enough for the children to each have one or to share in small groups.
4. Make a sample project for the children to follow.

Directions for Student:
1. Paste the engine at the left side of the paper bag.
2. Draw seven cars following the engine using the stencils.
3. Use a black crayon to make wheels and a track.
4. Write one day of the week on each car in the right order.

Monday

ENGINE PATTERN

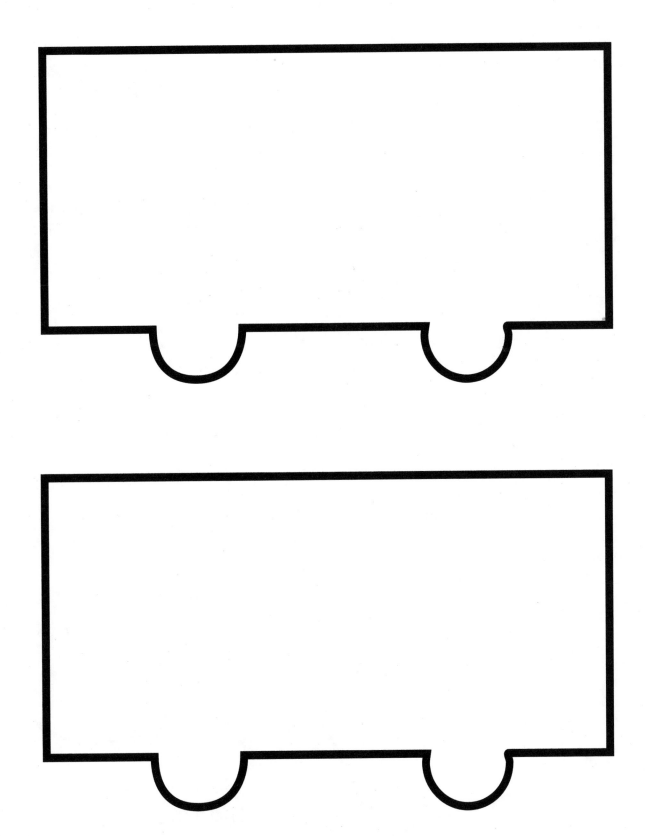

A DAY IN THE LIFE

SECOND GRADE

Objective: To concentrate on real occurrences and summarize them in written form.

Materials: large paper sacks (one per child), pencils, crayons, scissors, markers

Construction:
1. Cut the paper sacks along the seam to make flat working surfaces.
2. Give the papers to the students and show them how to fold the sacks so they're divided into four sections.
3. Tell the students that they will be writing about a day in their life.
4. Discuss and model the process with a sample of your own on the blackboard or on a large piece of butcher paper.

Directions for Student:
1. Think about how you spent yesterday. Remember what you did in the morning, at lunch time, in the afternoon, and before bed.
2. Write a few sentences in each section describing how you spent the day.
3. Illustrate the sentences.
4. Share your story with the class.

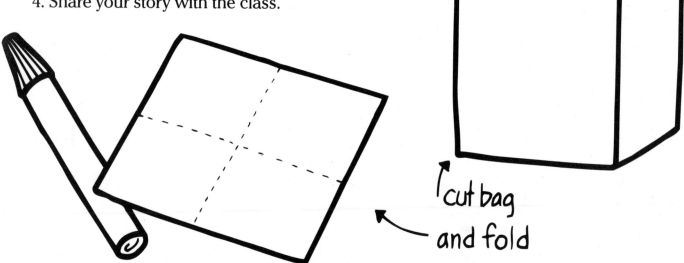

cut bag and fold

60

PERSONAL TIME LINE

THIRD GRADE

Objective: To reinforce personal importance and achievements.

Materials: paper bags (one per student), yardsticks (to be shared by students), achievement patterns (pg. 62), markers, scissors

Construction:
1. Duplicate the achievement patterns.
2. Let the children use the patterns as starters for their time lines if they are having difficulty brainstorming original ideas.

Directions for Student:
1. Cut the paper bag to make a flat surface.
2. Use a yardstick to help draw a straight line across the lower half of the flat paper bag.
3. Brainstorm 10 or more important events in your life to chart on the time line. Examples: losing your baby teeth, learning to ride a bike or roller skate, going on a trip, visiting relatives, etc. (If you get stuck, you can use the achievement patterns that apply to your life.)
4. Write these events down in the correct order on your time line.
5. Share the time line with your classmates.

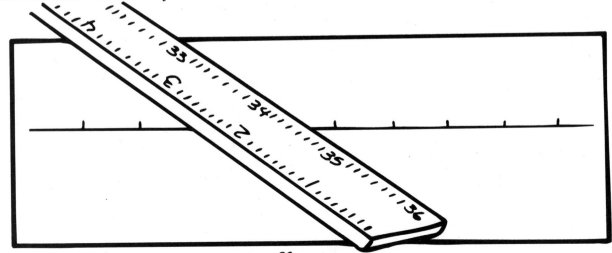

61

ACHIEVEMENT PATTERNS

CHAPTER SEVEN

EMPTY BOXES

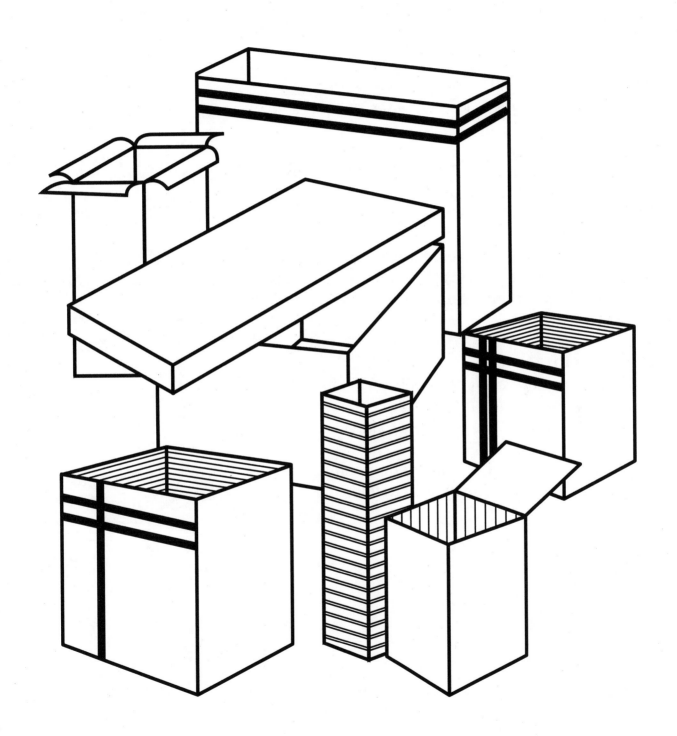

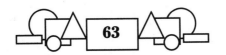

TREASURE BOX SEQUENCING

KINDERGARTEN

Objective: To reinforce mastery of big, medium, and small.

Materials: a set of different-size boxes with lids or closable flats that fit inside each other, pennies

Construction:
1. Hide a shiny penny as the treasure in the smallest box.
2. Enclose that box in a slightly larger one.
3. Put that box in another box, and continue until the treasure is six or seven boxes deep.
4. When a child has completed the activity and has lined up the boxes, give the child another penny to place inside the smallest box. Then set up the boxes for the next child to use.

Directions for Student:
1. Carefully remove each box until you get to the treasure in the smallest box. You may keep the treasure.
2. Line the boxes up from smallest to largest, and show the teacher.
3. When the teacher gives you another penny, place it in the smallest box for the next child to find.

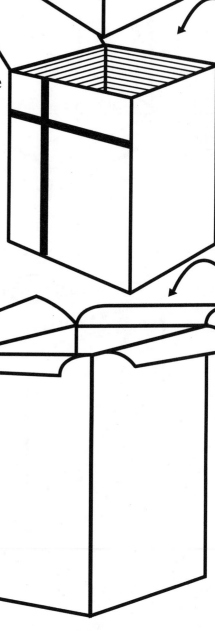

WHAT AM I?

FIRST GRADE

Objective: To write mini "mysteries" based on real objects.

Materials: a set of six or eight same-size small boxes, a variety of small items to spark imaginative stories or "mystery patterns" (pgs. 66-67), construction paper, scissors, writing paper, pencils

Construction:
1. Place five mystery items in each box. If using the mystery patterns, duplicate onto colored construction paper, cut them out, laminate, and place five in each box.
2. Set the boxes out on a table.

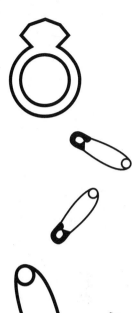

Directions for Student:
1. Choose a box and look at the items inside.
2. Think of something interesting about each item. You might imagine who could have owned the items, where they've been (in someone's pockets, on a beach, in the garbage), or how the items were made.
3. Write one or two sentences about each item, describing the object and inviting a reader to guess what the item is.
4. Share your paper with the rest of the class. See if anyone can guess the items from your clues.

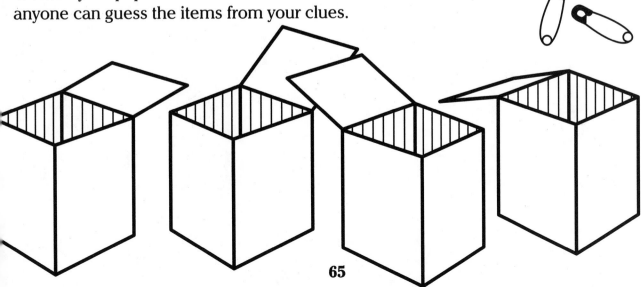

MYSTERY PATTERNS

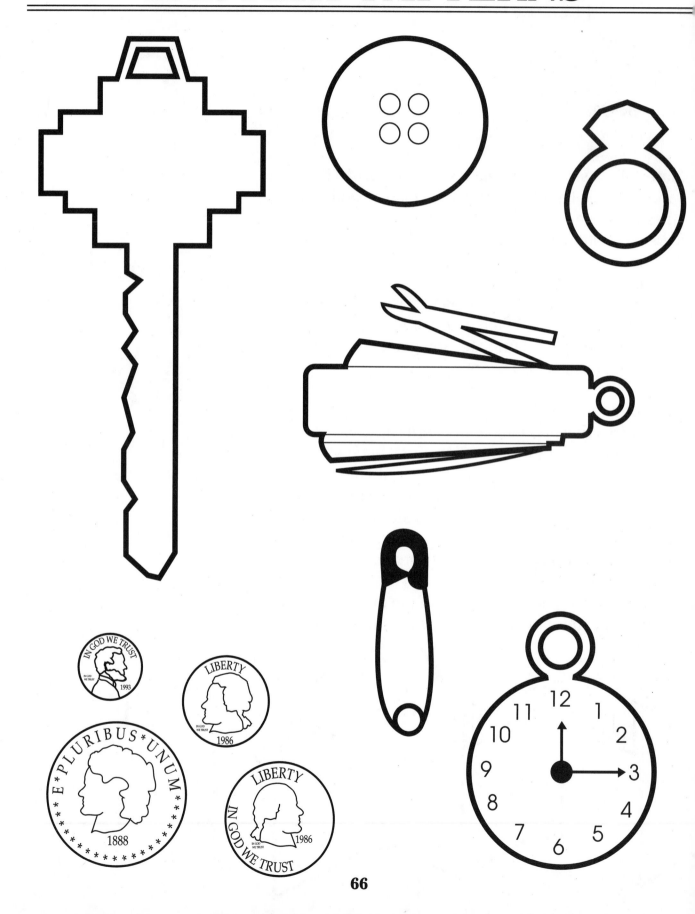

MYSTERY PATTERNS

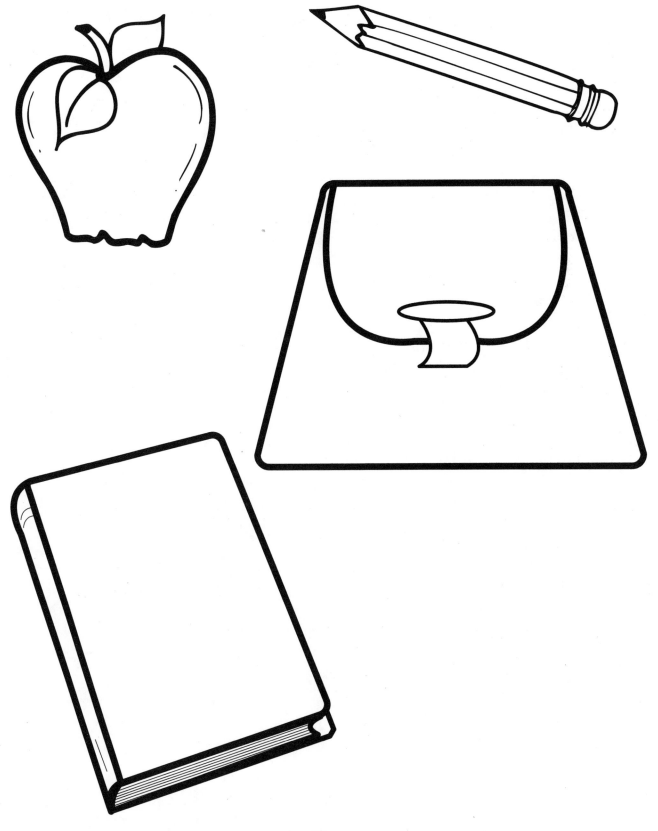

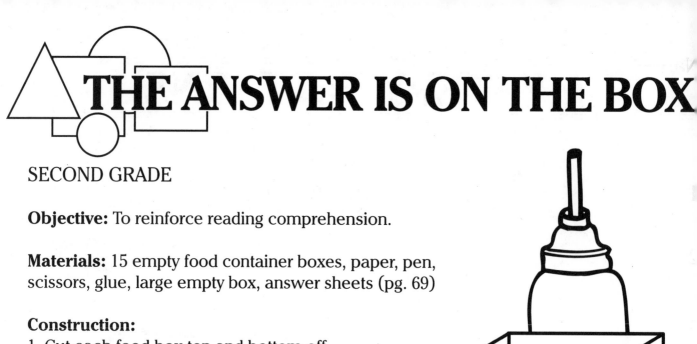

THE ANSWER IS ON THE BOX

SECOND GRADE

Objective: To reinforce reading comprehension.

Materials: 15 empty food container boxes, paper, pen, scissors, glue, large empty box, answer sheets (pg. 69)

Construction:
1. Cut each food box top and bottom off.
2. Cut each box on one folded side only so that it can be flattened to look like a folder.
3. Write five questions for each box on a sheet of paper, making sure that the answers can be found somewhere on the box. Examples:

- How long do you bake the cupcakes?
- How many eggs are needed?
- At what temperature do you set the oven?
- How many grams of fat are in one serving?

4. Glue each question sheet to the inside of the appropriate box "folder."
5. Laminate the boxes and give each a number.
6. Duplicate an answer sheet for each box and give the answer sheets corresponding numbers for the students to use to check themselves.
7. Store the boxes in a large empty box.

Directions for Student:
1. Take one box at a time and read the questions.
2. Find the answers by reading the information given on the box.
3. Record your answers on an answer sheet.

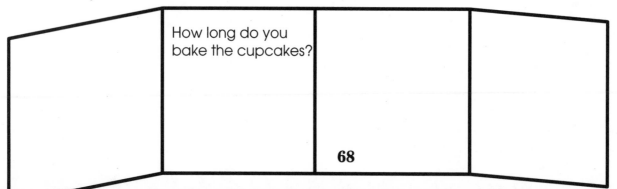

How long do you bake the cupcakes?

Name: _____

THE ANSWER IS ON THE BOX!

1. _____
   _____
2. _____
   _____
3. _____
   _____
4. _____
   _____
5. _____
   _____

Name: _____

THE ANSWER IS ON THE BOX!

1. _____
   _____
2. _____
   _____
3. _____
   _____
4. _____
   _____
5. _____
   _____

CREATE AND WRITE

THIRD GRADE

Objective: To write a short story based on a craft project.

Materials: boxes of different sizes and shapes (one per child), construction paper scraps, glue, markers, writing paper, pencils, scissors

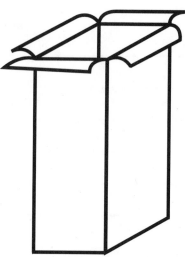

Construction:
No preparation work is necessary for this activity.

Directions for Student:
1. Create a building by gluing construction paper cutouts to a box. You can make a house, school, bank, post office, barn, store, bus depot, etc.
2. Write a short story about what might happen in your building. Your story can be about a day in the "life" of the building, written from the building's point of view, or about a special occurrence there, written from your own point of view or by an imaginary character.
3. Read your story to the class, showing the building and pointing out its importance to the story.

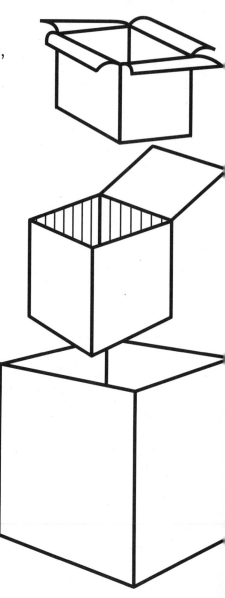

CHAPTER EIGHT

OUTDATED CALENDARS

SENTENCE/PICTURE MATCH

KINDERGARTEN

Objective: To reinforce vocabulary skills.

Materials: old calendar with pictures of distinctive objects (animals, specific buildings, foods), tagboard strips, markers, plastic bag, scissors

Construction:
1. On each tagboard strip, write a short sentence that fits the pictures in the calendar, keeping in mind the reading vocabulary of your class.
2. Write six to eight picture sentences to match. As children progress, work up to all twelve.
3. Cut out the pictures.
4. Store the strips and the pictures in a plastic bag.

Directions for Student:
1. Spread out the pictures.
2. Read each sentence out loud, or have the teacher or another person read them to you.
3. Match the sentences with the pictures.

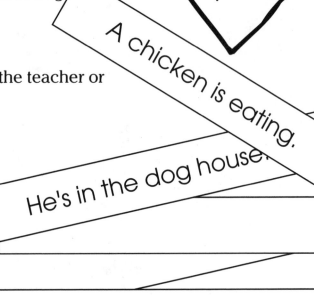

A chicken is eating.

He's in the dog house.

It is time for a nap.

Let's go for a walk.

FIND IT ON THE CALENDAR

FIRST GRADE

Objective: To learn how to use a calendar.

Materials: calendars (one per child), worksheets (pg. 74; one per child), pencils

Construction:
No preparation work is needed for this activity.

Directions for Student:
1. Use the calendar to find the answers to the questions on the worksheet.
2. Exchange your paper with another student and check your answers. If you do not agree on an answer, check with another student or with the teacher.

January 1994

Sunday	Monday	Tuesday	Wednesday	Thursday	Friday	Saturday
						1
2	3	4	5	6	7	8
9	10	11	12	13	14	15
16	17	18	19	20	21	22
23	24	25	26	27	28	29
30	31					

FIND IT ON THE CALENDAR

1. How many days are in this month?

_____

2. How many Sundays are there?

_____

3. What day of the week is the 11th?

_____

4. What date is the second Tuesday?

_____

5. How many Fridays are there?

_____

6. What day of the week is the 25th?

_____

7. What is the date of the third Monday?

_____

8. How many Wednesdays are there?

_____

9. What date is the first Friday?

_____

10. What is the last day of this month?

_____

CREATIVE WRITING BOOKS

SECOND GRADE

Objective: To make take-home illustrated books.

Materials: spiral-bound calendars with a picture for each month (one per student), scissors, stapler, lined writing paper

Construction:
1. Cut the lined paper to fit over the calendar part of each page.
2. Staple the four corners to cover the calendar section. Do this for all twelve months of each calendar. Each calendar is now a book of twelve pictures with a piece of writing paper under each picture.
3. Pass out the calendars to be used during story writing sessions. The calendars will last for twelve sessions, and will then be books of twelve "illustrated" stories to take home.

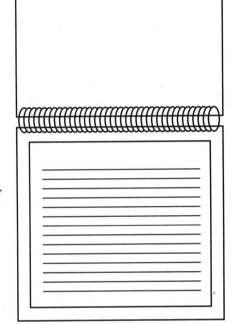

Directions for Student:
1. Choose one of the pictures in the booklet and study it.
2. Write a short story about the picture on the paper below it.

Option: When the students have completed the book, they may want to make another one using calendar pictures of subjects they're especially interested in.

READING LOG

THIRD GRADE

Objective: To practice writing summaries while keeping track of books read.

Materials: spiral-bound calendars (one per child), lined paper, scissors, stapler, marker

Construction:
1. Cut the paper to fit over the calendar part of each page.
2. Staple the paper over each calendar section.
3. On the first page of each log, write in the month that school starts, and continue with the months in sequence through the rest of the year.
4. Give each child a calendar at the beginning of the school year.

Directions for Student:
1. Record all the books that you read in each particular month.
2. Write a short summary beneath each title.
3. Share your reading log with another student, and choose a book to read from his or her list.
4. At the end of the school year, take the reading log home to log books that you read during the summer.

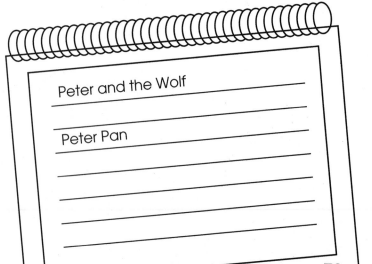

Peter and the Wolf

Peter Pan

CHAPTER NINE

OLD NEWSPAPERS

MY NAME COLLAGE

KINDERGARTEN

Objective: To practice spelling names.

Materials: newspapers with headlines in large-sized type (enough for a whole class to use), scissors, manila paper (one sheet per student), glue

Construction:
1. Give each child a section of the newspaper.
2. Help the children spell their names. Also help them find the letters in their names, if they need assistance.

Directions for Student:
1. Find the letters in your name in the newspaper headlines and cut them out.
2. Glue the cut-out letters onto the paper to spell your name.

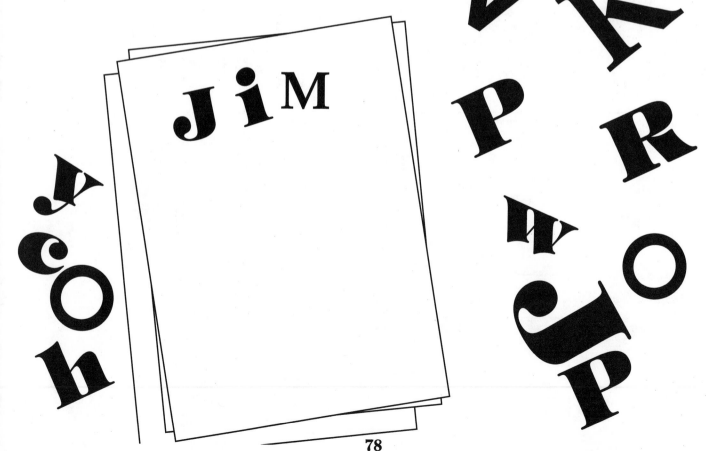

COMIC STRIP SEQUENCING

FIRST GRADE

Objective: To reinforce comprehension skills.

Materials: five comic strips, five pieces of construction paper in different colors, scissors, glue, plastic bag

Construction:
1. Cut the comic strips apart and glue the panels from the same comic strip on slightly larger pieces of the same color of construction paper.
2. Follow this process for all five comic strips.
3. Laminate all the cards.
4. Store all the pieces in the plastic bag.

Directions for Student:
1. Take out the pieces and sort them into color piles.
2. Arrange the individual comic strip sections in the correct sequence to tell the cartoon's story.

Option: This activity can also be done as a class project. Pass out all the pieces and have the students get in color groups. Let them sequence their own set of cards and read the completed comic to the class.

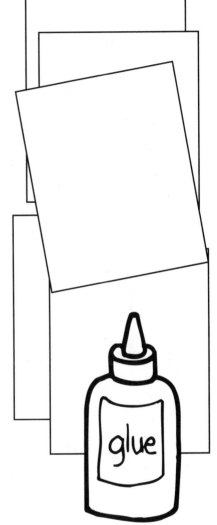

READ FOR THE MAIN IDEA

SECOND GRADE

Objective: To reinforce reading comprehension.

Materials: newspapers, tagboard, scissors, glue, large plastic bag

Construction:
1. Cut out newspaper articles that will be interesting to your students and easy enough for them to read.
2. Cut the headline off each article.
3. Glue the headlines and the articles onto separate pieces of tagboard.
4. Laminate all the pieces and store in a plastic bag.

Directions for Student:
1. Take out all of the news articles and the headline strips.
2. Read each article and think about what the main idea is.
3. Match the correct headline strip with each article.

Option: To do this as a group activity, pass out one article to each student. Give the children time to read their articles silently. When you call out a headline, have the student who has that article bring it forward, or read it to the class.

Elephants at the Zoo

Elephants at the Zoo

Young Boy Climbs Mountain

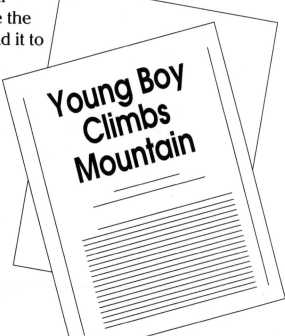

Young Boy Climbs Mountain

WRITE ABOUT THE HEADLINES

THIRD GRADE

Objective: To reinforce reading comprehension.

Materials: newspapers, scissors, writing paper, pencils, manila folders, glue, newspaper pattern (pg. 82)

Construction:
1. Duplicate one newspaper pattern for each child.
2. Cut out headlines from old newspapers, making sure that your students understand the words in the headlines.
3. Pass out headlines and the patterns to the students.
4. Once students have written their articles and glued the articles with the headlines to a folder, place the real article in each folder.
5. Have the students read each other's stories and then compare them to the real articles.

The Daily Gazette

Directions for Student:
1. Read the newspaper headline.
2. Glue the newspaper pattern to the front of a manila folder.
3. On the pattern, write a short article that would be appropriate for the headline. Use the photo box for an illustration if you'd like.
4. Glue the headline into the space above your story and give the folder to your teacher.
5. Read another student's story that the teacher gives you and compare it to the original newspaper article inside the folder.

Cat Climbs Telephone Pole

President

Teacher

7-Year-Old Girl Wins Race

✳✳✳The Daily Gazette✳✳✳

ISSUE 1

25 cents

CHAPTER TEN

WRAPPING PAPER

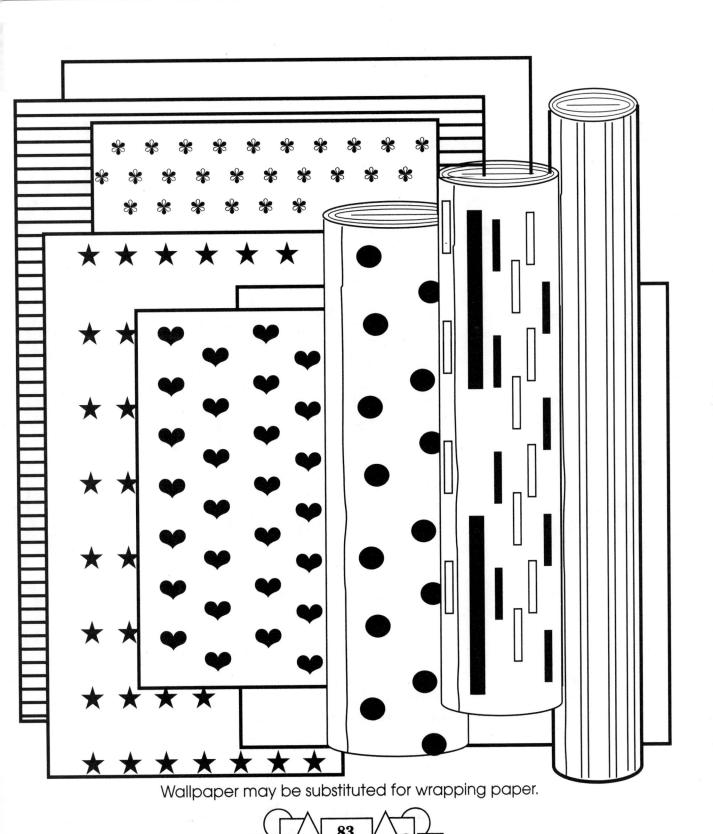

Wallpaper may be substituted for wrapping paper.

ABC FOOTPRINTS

KINDERGARTEN

Objective: To practice the ABCs in upper- and lower-case.

Materials: long strip of 6- to 8-inch-wide tagboard, wrapping paper, scissors, marker or upper-case alphabet stencils, footprint patterns (pg. 85), plastic bag

Construction:
1. Cut 26 wrapping paper footprints using the patterns provided.
2. Write or stencil an upper-case alphabet letter on each footprint.
3. Laminate the footprints. Store in a plastic bag.
4. Write lower-case alphabet letters in order on the strip of tagboard far enough apart for a footprint to be lined up under each letter.
5. When a student is ready to use this activity, scramble the footprints and lay the tagboard strip on the floor.

Directions for Student:
1. Match the letters on the footprints to the letters written on the tagboard.
2. Have the teacher check your work when you have finished.

FOOTPRINT PATTERNS

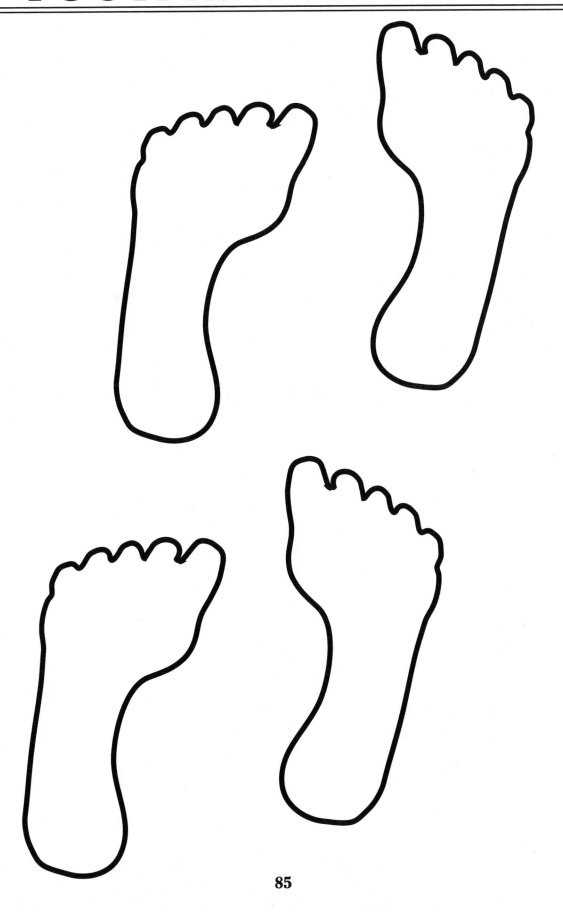

ABBREVIATIONS

FIRST GRADE

Objective: To teach the abbreviations for the months and the days of the week.

Materials: ice cream cone and scoop patterns (pg. 87), brown or tan construction paper, a variety of decorated gift-wrapping paper, scissors, marker, plastic bag, writing paper, pencils

Construction:
1. Use the patterns to cut 19 "cones" from brown or tan construction paper and 19 "scoops" from the wrapping paper.
2. Write the long form of the months and the days of the week on the cone shapes.
3. Write the corresponding abbreviations on the scoops.
4. Laminate all the pieces and cut them out.
5. Store the pieces in a plastic bag.

Directions for Student:
1. Spread the cones on a flat surface and match the correct scoop abbreviation with the correct cone shape.
2. Write the words and their abbreviations on a piece of paper and give it to the teacher to check.

ICE CREAM CONE
AND SCOOP PATTERNS

BEGINNING/ENDING SENTENCE MATCH

SECOND GRADE

Objective: To reinforce understanding of sentence structure.

Materials: assorted patterns of gift-wrapping paper cut in 3" x 12" strips, sample sentences (pg. 89), scissors, tagboard, glue, markers, one large plastic bag

Construction:
1. Duplicate a two-part sentence on the back of each wrapping paper strip.
2. Laminate the sentence strips and cut them out.
3. Cut the strips in half, forming a beginning and an ending segment as shown on the patterns.
4. Store the strips in the plastic bag.

Directions for Student:
1. Sort the sentence strips into beginning and ending parts.
2. Spread out all the beginning sentence segments and quickly read through them. Do the same thing with the ending segments.
3. Place the correct ending sentence segment beside each beginning segment to make complete sentences.
4. Check your work by turning the sentences over and seeing if the wrapping paper patterns match.

The funny clown   sold us balloons.

SAMPLE SENTENCES

The little boy	played with his bat and ball.
At 6:00 a.m. the farmer	milked the cow.
The bus driver	stopped the bus at my house.
On my birthday, the baker	baked a big chocolate cake.
The experienced astronaut	got out of the spaceship first.
The music teacher	taught us a new song.
The basketball player	shot baskets after school.
The funny clown	made us laugh.
The doctor and nurse	worked at the hospital.
Today the mail carrier	delivered the mail.

SENTENCE SEQUENCING

THIRD GRADE

Objective: To reinforce understanding of sentence structure.

Materials: 10 different patterns of gift-wrapping paper, scissors, markers, plastic bag, writing paper, pencils

Construction:
1. Cut 2- x 10-inch strips of different patterns of wrapping paper.
2. Write a simple six-word sentence on the blank side of each strip.
3. Cut apart the sentences between the words.
4. Laminate the word cards.
5. Put all the pieces in the bag.

Directions for Student:
1. Spread the word cards on a flat surface.
2. Sort the cards according to the patterns.
3. Arrange the words to make the sentences read correctly.
4. Write the sentences on a piece of paper and turn it in for the teacher to check.

school

walks

Mary

day.

every

to

Mary walks to school every day.

CHAPTER ELEVEN

POPSICLE STICKS

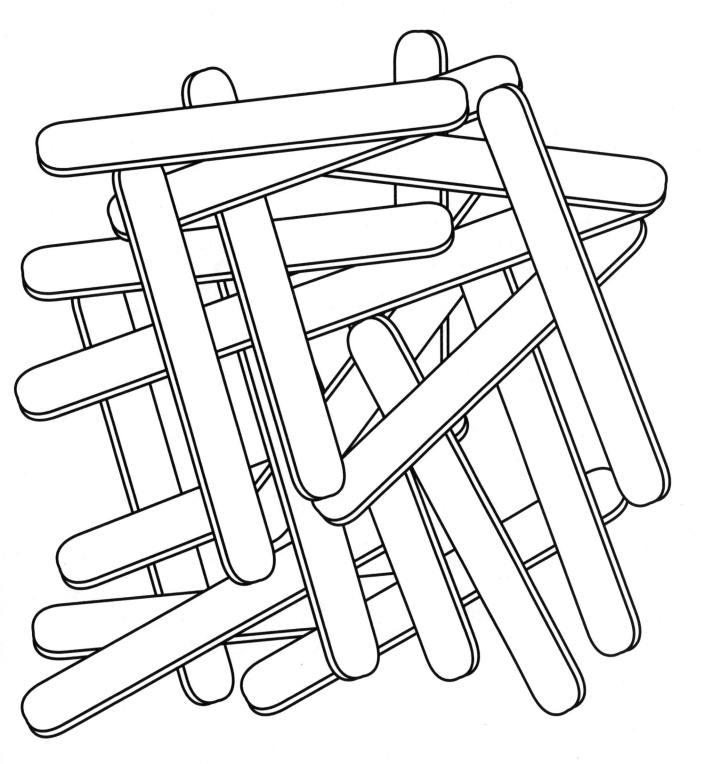

RHYMING WORDS

KINDERGARTEN

Objective: To practice reading skills and to understand what makes words rhyme.

Materials: 20 Popsicle sticks for each set, rhyming word sets (pg. 93), colored markers, plastic bags, glue

Construction:
1. Write a rhyming word on each Popsicle stick.
2. Store each set of Popsicle sticks in a separate bag.

Directions for Student:
1. Empty the bag onto a flat surface.
2. Sort the sticks into groups of rhyming words.

Option: If the children cannot read, have an aide read the words to them. Then have the students choose the rhyming words by the sound.

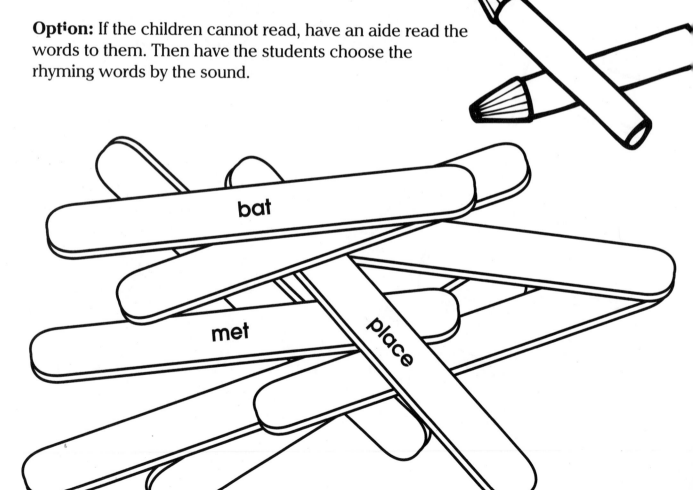

RHYMING WORD SETS

Set One:

cat

bat

hat

mat

sat

Set Two:

bed

red

led

fed

sled

Set Three:

face

lace

place

race

space

Set Four:

pet

met

net

set

bet

SEQUENCE THE MONTHS

FIRST GRADE

Objective: To practice naming the months in the correct order.

Materials: 12 Popsicle sticks for each set made, month patterns (pg. 95), glue, plastic bags, scissors, marker

Construction:
1. Duplicate the month patterns and cut them apart.
2. Glue one month on each Popsicle stick.
3. Write a number (from 1 to 12) on the back of each stick, starting with 1 for January.
4. Store the sticks in a plastic bag.

Note: If you are making more than one set, duplicate the names of the months onto different colors of paper. This will eliminate any mix-up between the sets.

Directions for Student:
1. Take out all the sticks.
2. Arrange the months in the correct order.
3. Turn the Popsicle sticks over and check the numbers to see if you have put the months in the correct order.

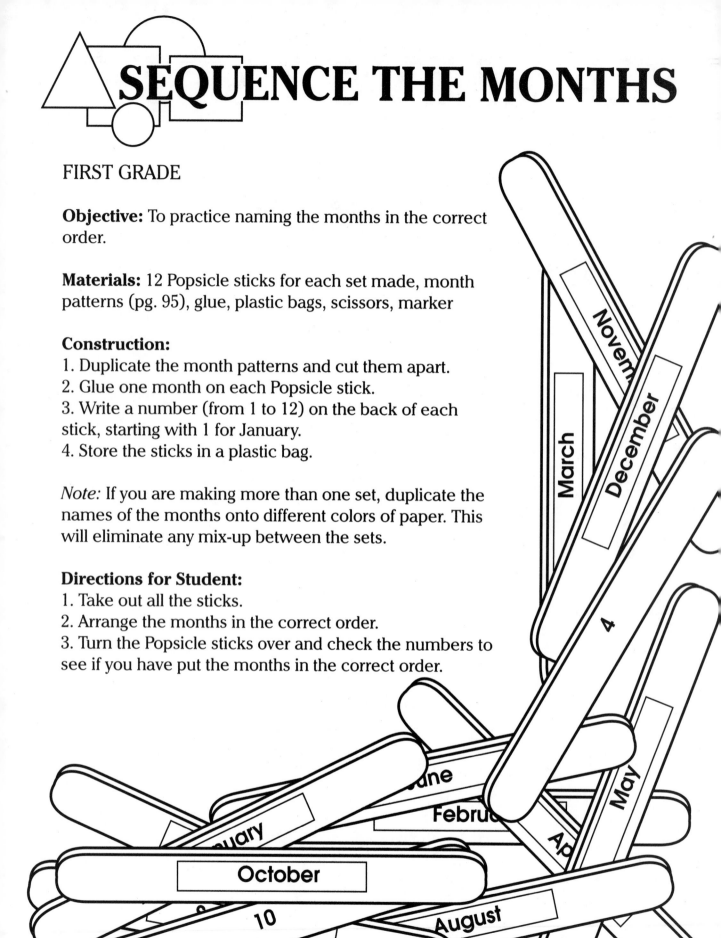

94

MONTH PATTERNS

January	January	January
February	February	February
March	March	March
April	April	April
May	May	May
June	June	June
July	July	July
August	August	August
September	September	September
October	October	October
November	November	November
December	December	December

SHORT STORY SEQUENCING

SECOND GRADE

Objective: To reinforce the understanding of story sequence.

Materials: 30 Popsicle sticks, sample stories (pg. 97), fine-tipped markers in five different colors, plastic bag

Construction:
1. Write the title of a story with one of the markers on one Popsicle stick. Use all capital letters for the title.
2. Using the same color marker, write a sentence on each of five more Popsicle sticks that together tell the story.
3. Write four more titles and five-sentence stories with the other markers.
4. Store all the Popsicle sticks in a plastic bag.

Directions for Student:
1. Spread out the Popsicle sticks and sort them by color.
2. Choose one color to start with, and put that story's title at the top. You will know it's the title because it will be in all capital letters.
3. Read the rest of the sticks in that color, and arrange them in order to put the short story in correct sequence.
4. Continue until all five short stories are completed.

Option: To do this as a class activity, divide the students into groups of six. Give each group a plastic bag with one complete story told on Popsicle sticks. Have the students arrange themselves in order to read their story to the class. (One child reads the title, the next reads the first sentence, and so on.)

Then apples began growing.

I wrote the letter a

MY APPLE TREE

ped it.

I put the letter in the mailbox.

Sam got my letter.

My friend Sam was at camp.

SAMPLE STORIES

The Letter
My friend Sam was at camp.
I wanted to write him a letter.
I wrote the letter and stamped it.
I put the letter in the mailbox.
Two days later, Sam got my letter.

My Apple Tree
Winter was over, and spring had arrived.
The branches on my apple tree grew leaves.
Tiny white and pink buds formed.
Then apples began growing.
One day, the apples were ripe enough to eat!

Shopping
My mom took me shopping for school clothes.
We found a lot of nice things for me.
I tried them all on to make sure they fit.
Mom paid for the ones we wanted to buy.
I took the clothes home and put them in my closet.

ALPHABETICAL ORDER BY THIRD LETTER

THIRD GRADE

Objective: To practice alphabetization skills.

Materials: 24 Popsicle sticks, markers, plastic bag, writing paper, pencils

Construction:
1. Write one word on each Popsicle stick.
2. Store the sticks in a plastic bag.

Directions for Student:
1. Spread out the Popsicle sticks. Arrange the words on the sticks alphabetically according to the first three letters of each word.
2. Write the words in alphabetical order on a piece of paper and turn it in for the teacher to check.

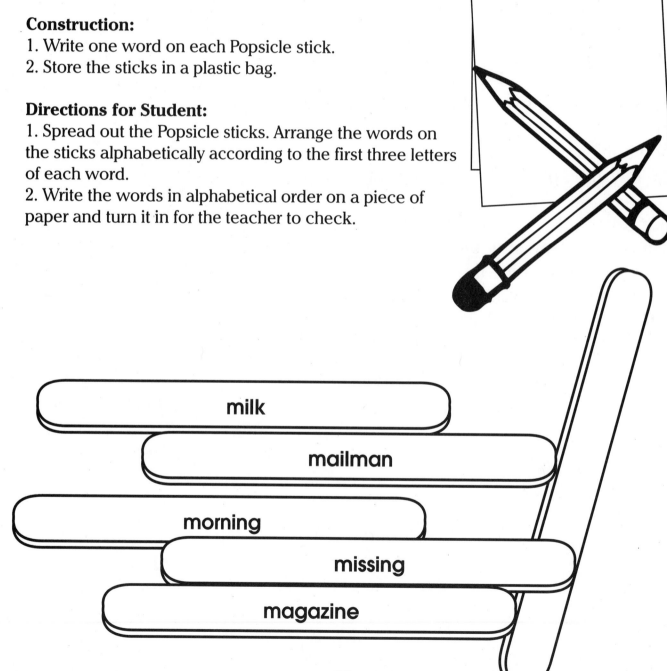

milk

mailman

morning

missing

magazine

98

CHAPTER TWELVE

EGG CARTONS

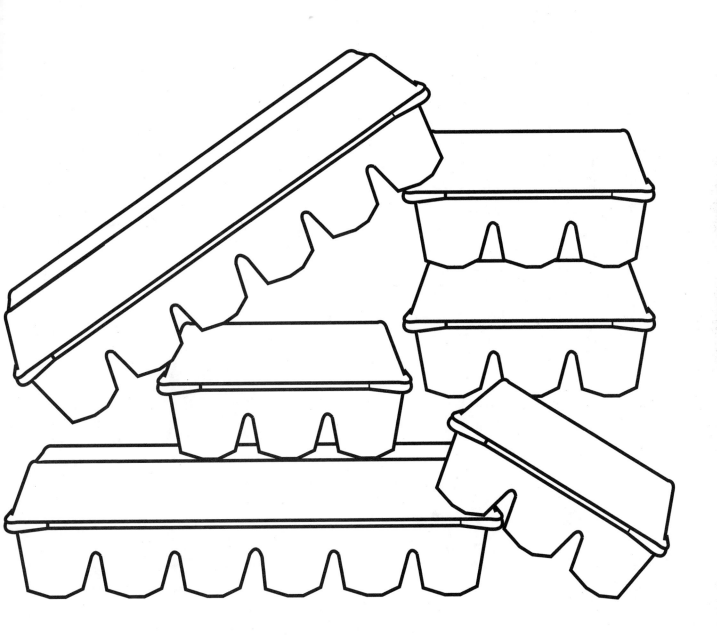

COLOR WORD MATCH

KINDERGARTEN

Objective: To practice color word recognition.

Materials: cardboard egg carton, picture cards (pg. 101), word cards (pg. 102), white glue, water, brush, scissors, plastic bag

Construction:
1. Duplicate the picture cards, laminate, and cut out.
2. Cut out the word cards and put one into each section of the egg carton.
3. Use a paintbrush to smear a mixture of white glue and water over each word for a more permanent finish.
4. Store the picture cards in a plastic bag.

Directions for Student:
1. Take out all the picture cards.
2. Look at the color words in the egg carton.
3. Put the corresponding picture card in the correct section. For example, the snowman will go in the white section.

Option: For children who cannot read, place a dab of the color beneath each color word.

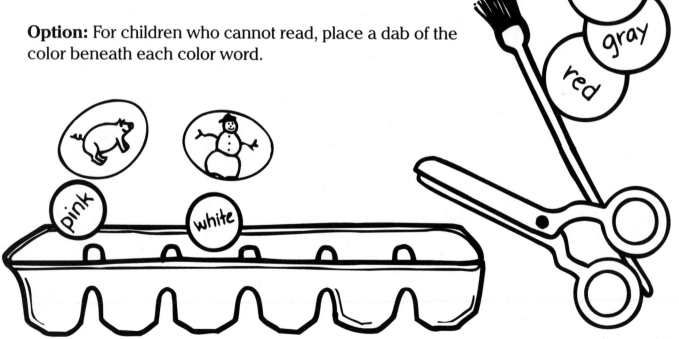

PICTURE CARDS

WORD CARDS

red

orange

yellow

green

blue

purple

white

black

gray

brown

pink

silver

MATCH NOUNS AND ADJECTIVES

FIRST GRADE

Objective: To reinforce understanding of nouns and adjectives.

Materials: cardboard egg carton, noun cards (pg. 105), adjective cards (pg. 104), white glue, scissors, paintbrush, water

Construction:
1. Duplicate the noun cards, and cut them apart.
2. Duplicate the adjective cards, laminate, and cut them apart.
3. Glue a noun card into each egg carton section.
4. Paint white glue and water over the surface of the noun cards to make a more permanent finish.

Directions for Student:
1. Look at the nouns in the egg carton sections.
2. Put the egg-shaped adjective cards with the nouns in the appropriate sections.

ADJECTIVE CARDS

juicy

furry

soft

tall

funny

chocolate

silver

green

hot

rubber

heavy

pink

NOUN CARDS

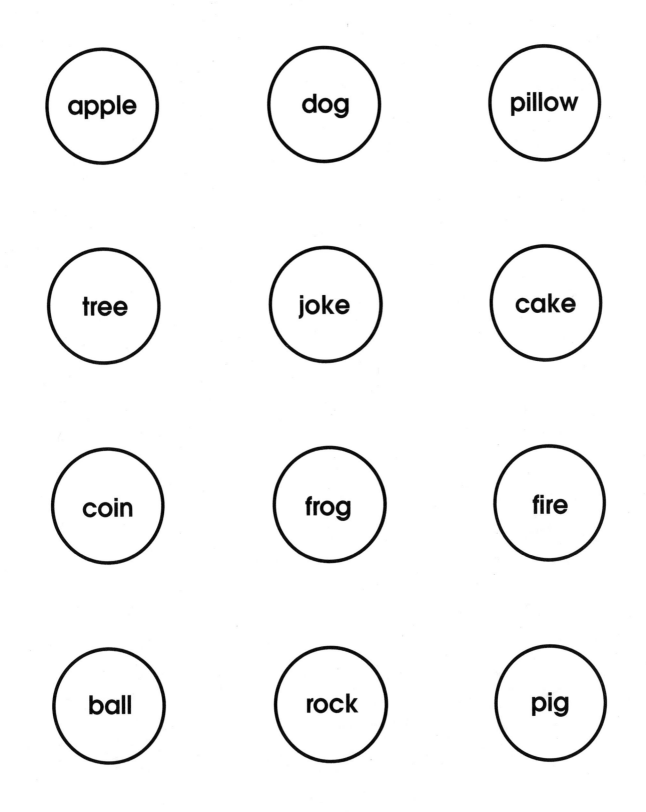

SYNONYM MATCH

SECOND GRADE

Objective: To practice synonym recognition.

Materials: cardboard egg carton, word cards and egg shapes (pg. 107), scissors, white glue, paintbrush, water

Construction:
1. Duplicate the word cards and egg shapes.
2. Cut out the word cards and glue one into each egg carton section.
3. Cut out the egg shapes and laminate them.
4. Paint white glue and water over the surface of the word cards to make a more permanent finish.

Directions for Student:
1. Look at each word card and find the two eggs that mean the same thing.
2. Put the egg shapes in the section with the matching word.

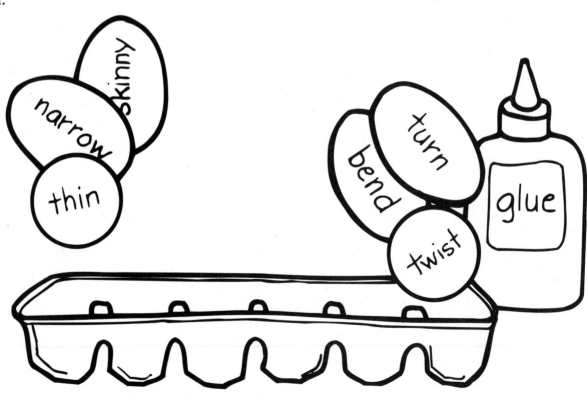

106

EGG SHAPES & WORD CARDS

hop

jump

rabbit

bunny

quick

fast

violet

lavender

narrow

skinny

pot

pan

turn

bend

small

tiny

afraid

frightened

fix

mend

stir

mix

neat

clean

leap

hare

swift

thin

kettle

twist

little

tidy

blend

repair

scared

purple

SYNONYMS AND ANTONYMS

THIRD GRADE

Objective: To study synonyms and antonyms in depth.

Materials: cardboard egg carton, word cards and egg shapes (pg. 109), glue, water, paintbrush, scissors

Construction:
1. Cut out the word cards and paste one in each egg carton section.
2. Paint over the surface with a mixture of water and glue to make a more permanent finish.
3. Laminate and cut out the egg shapes.

Directions for Student:
1. Look at each word in the egg carton sections and find an egg with a synonym and an egg with an antonym for it.
2. Place the egg shapes in the correct sections.

Option: Use the blank patterns (pg. 110) to make additional cards or to let students make their own cards.

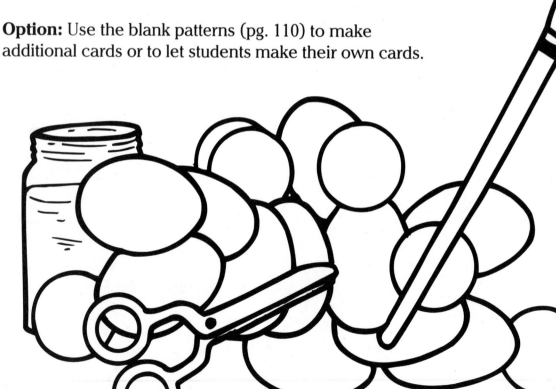

WORD CARDS & EGG SHAPES

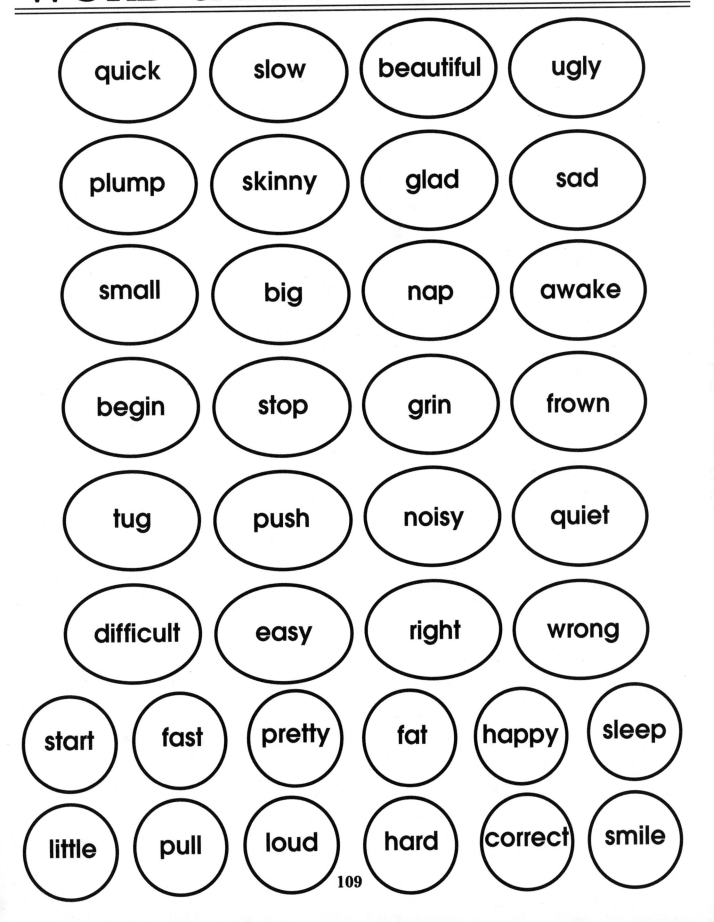

quick

slow

beautiful

ugly

plump

skinny

glad

sad

small

big

nap

awake

begin

stop

grin

frown

tug

push

noisy

quiet

difficult

easy

right

wrong

start

fast

pretty

fat

happy

sleep

little

pull

loud

hard

correct

smile

109

BLANK SHAPES

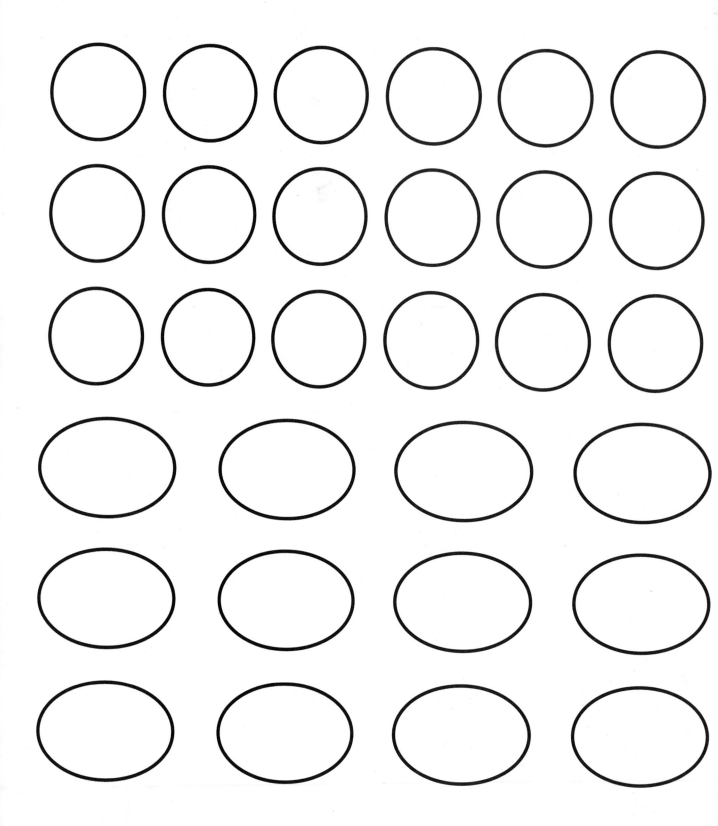

CHAPTER THIRTEEN

USED GREETING CARDS

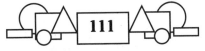

ALPHABET MATCHUP

KINDERGARTEN

Objective: To reinforce knowledge of the ABCs.

Materials: 26 greeting cards (pictures only—non-religious), ABC patterns (pgs. 113-125), marker, scissors, plastic bag, glue

Construction:
1. Paste one pattern for each letter of the alphabet to the back of a greeting card picture.
2. Cut the card in two sections.
3. Laminate all the cards and trim.
4. Store all the pieces in a plastic bag.

Directions for Student:
1. Find the upper- and lower-case letters for each alphabet letter and put the two "puzzle" pieces together.
2. If the letters are correct, the pieces will make a complete picture when turned over. If the match is not correct, the pictures will be different. You'll need to try again.

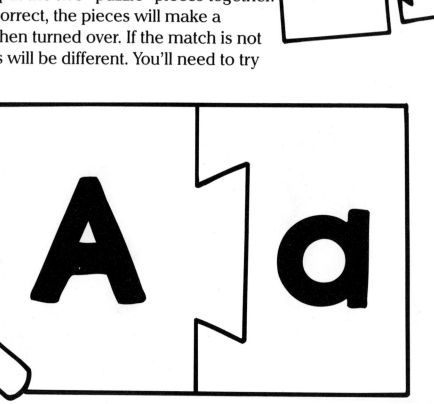

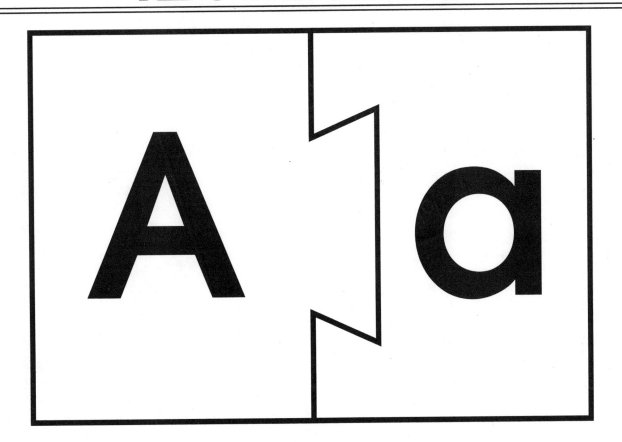

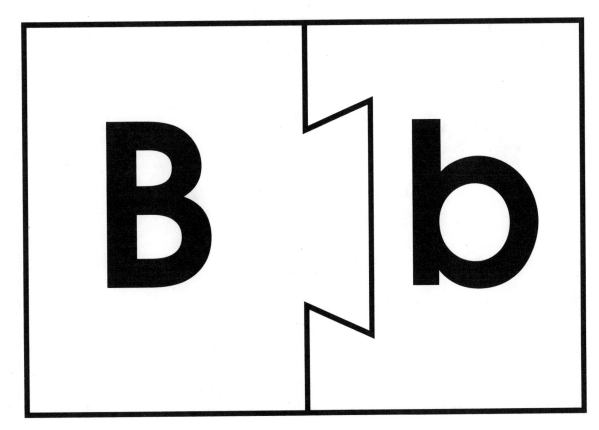

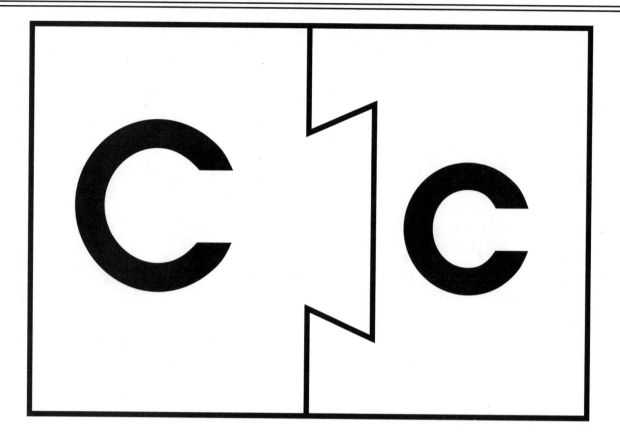

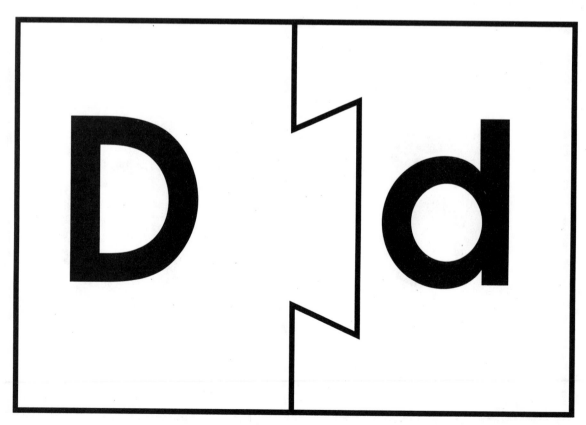

ABC PATTERNS

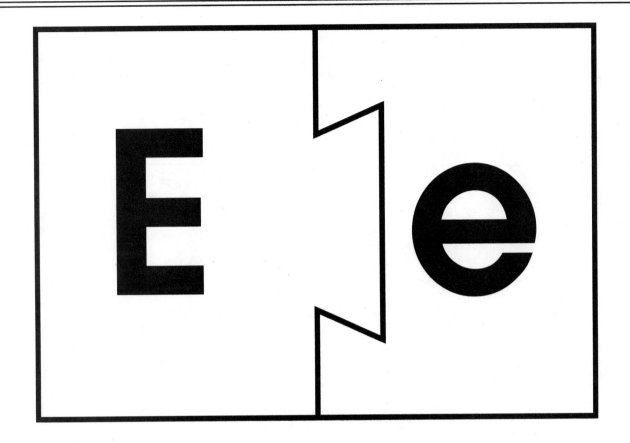

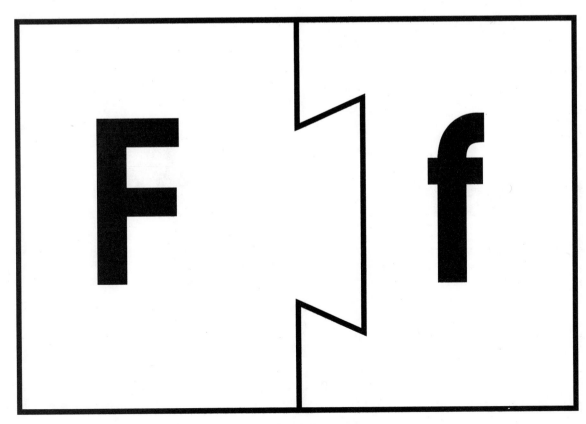

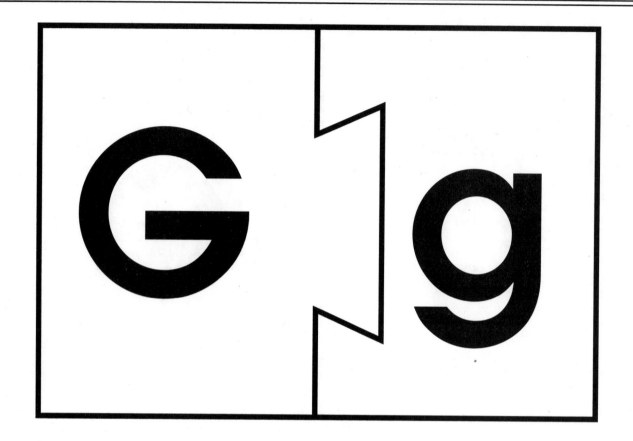

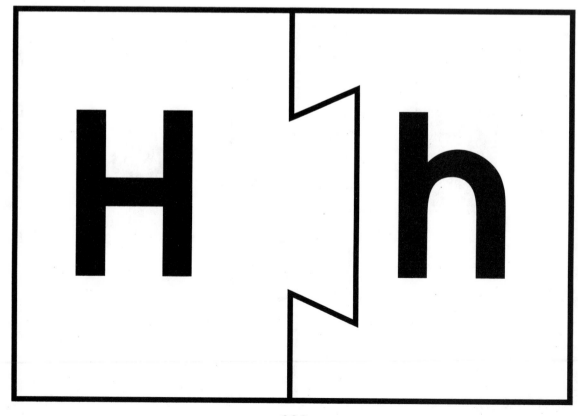

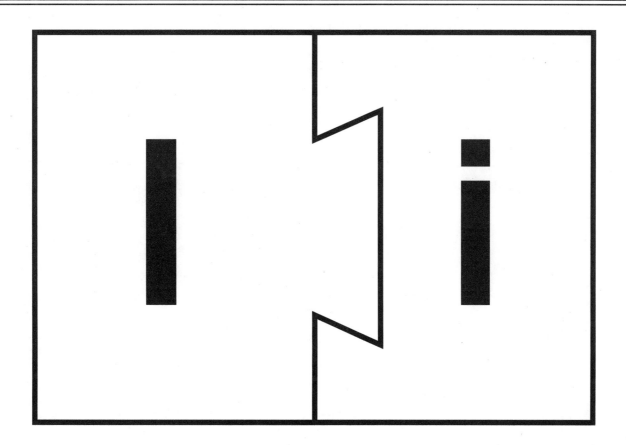

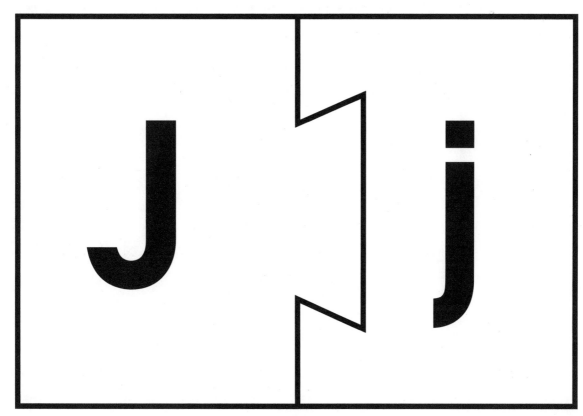

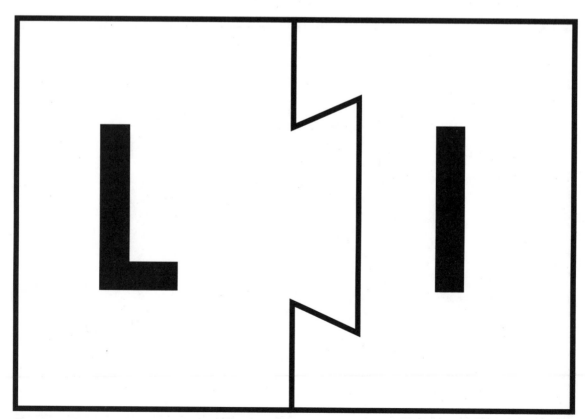

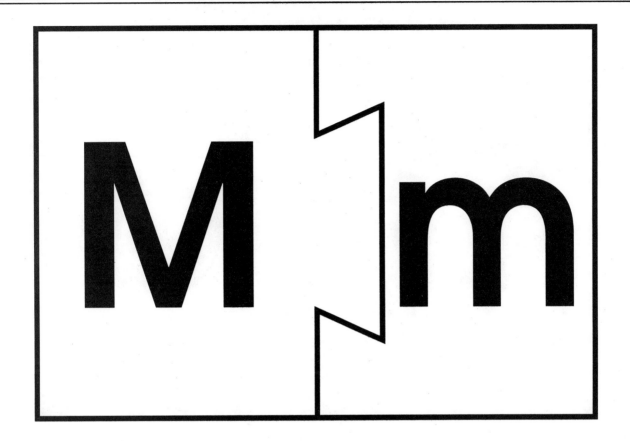

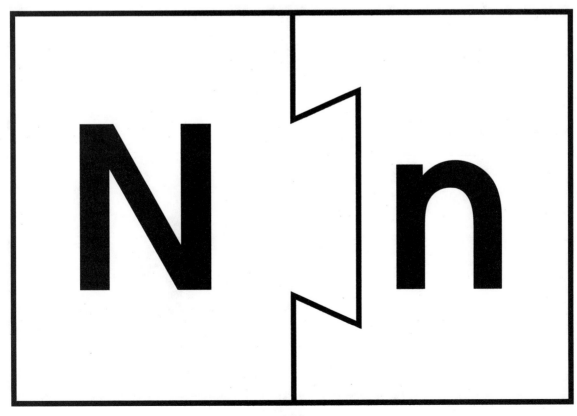

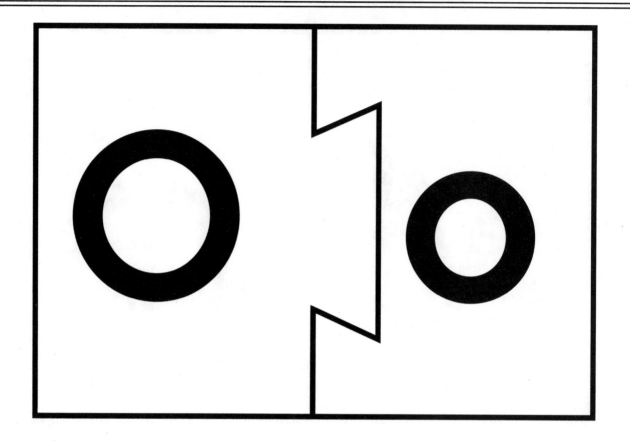

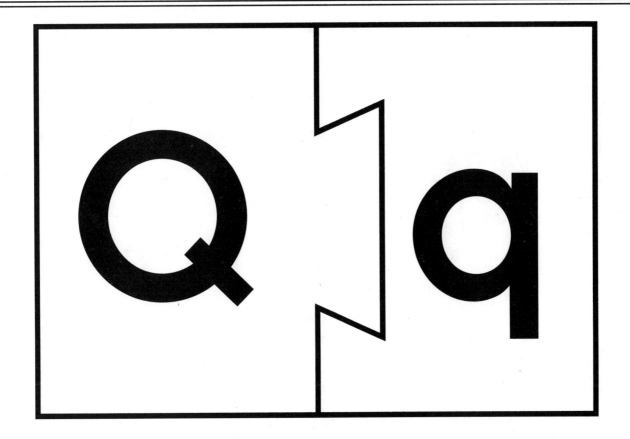

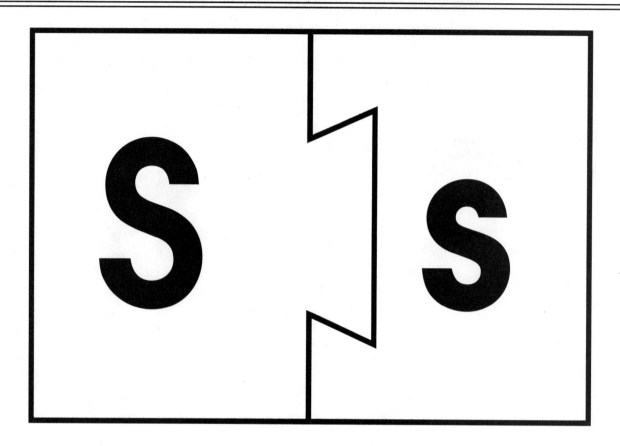

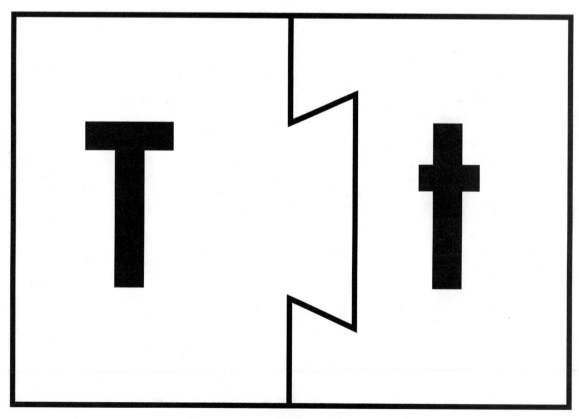

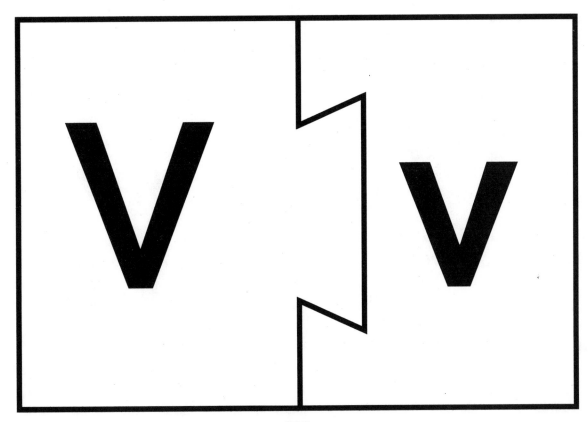

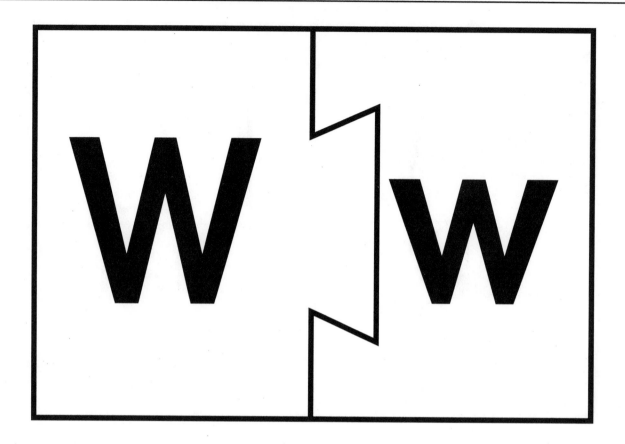

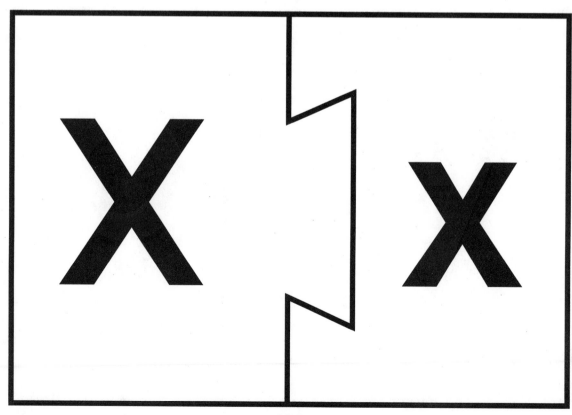

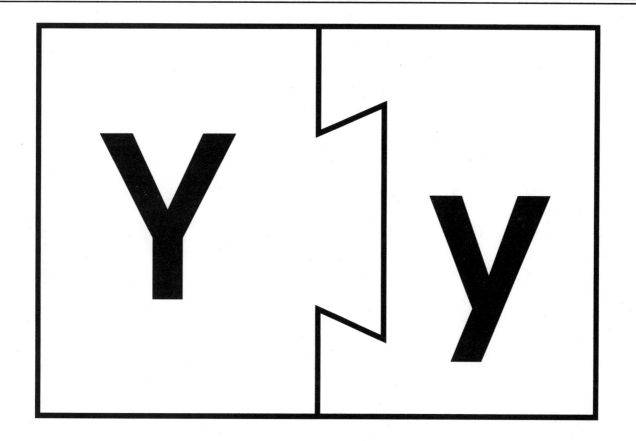

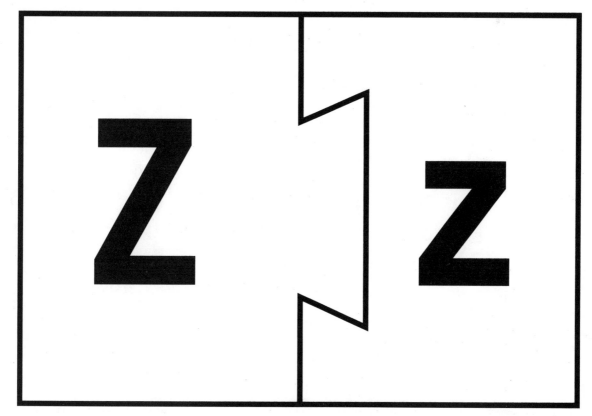

POST CARD PRETENDING

FIRST GRADE

Objective: To practice letter-writing skills.

Materials: used greeting cards (non-religious—one per child), marker, scissors, pencils

Construction:
1. Cut the greeting cards in half so that the students can use the picture part.
2. Draw a vertical line dividing the blank side of each card in half so it looks like a post card.
3. Divide the children into pairs for the writing assignment.
4. Deliver the students' notes after they're written.

Directions for Student:
1. Write a short note to your partner.
2. Give the card to the teacher, who will play mail carrier and deliver it.
3. If you'd like, write a reply note to the card you receive from your partner.

Mark,
Let's ride our bikes this Saturday.

from
Mary

To Mark

WRITE TO A CHARACTER

SECOND GRADE

Objective: To reinforce the concept of "character."

Materials: used greeting cards (non-religious—one per child), pencils, scissors

Construction:
1. Cut off the picture part of the greeting cards for student use.
2. Line the cards up along the chalkboard and let each student pick one.

Directions for Student:
1. Pick a card.
2. Write a note on the back of the card to a character in a book you've read in class.
3. Exchange cards with another student who's read the same book. Ask that person to write back from your character's point of view.

SEQUENCE THE STORY

THIRD GRADE

Objective: To reinforce reading comprehension.

Materials: picture side of five greeting cards, marker, scissors, plastic bags

Construction:
1. Write a four sentence short story on the plain side of each greeting card.
2. Laminate the cards and cut into strips.
3. Store each set of strips in a plastic bag.

Directions for Student:
1. Take the strips out of the bag and spread them out with the writing side facing up.
2. Arrange the strips in order so that the story makes sense.
3. Turn the pieces over, in the same order, to self-check. The story is complete if all the picture parts fit together.

John and Mary like to ride bikes.

One Saturday they rode to the park.

Then they had lunch.

After they ate, they rode home.